THE OFFICIAL **NATIONAL PARK GUIDE**

EXMOOR

Text and photographs by Brian Pearce

SERIES EDITOR **Roly Smith**

PEVENSEY GUIDES

The Pevensey Press is an imprint of
David & Charles

First published in the UK in 2001

Map artwork by Chartwell Illustrators
based on material supplied by the
Exmoor National Park Authority

A catalogue record for this book is
available from the British Library.

ISBN 1 898630 15 1

Book design by Les Dominey Design
Company, Exeter
and printed in Hong Kong by
Hong Kong Graphics and
Printing Ltd
for David & Charles
Brunel House Newton Abbot Devon

Contents

Page 1: The Exe valley near Dulverton
Pages 2 and 3: The Vale of Porlock from Crawter Hill (courtesy National Trust)
Left: Elwill Bay
Front cover: (above) Woody Bay; (below) Malmsmead; (front flap) Porlock Weir
Back cover: (above) The Valley of Rocks; (below) Selworthy

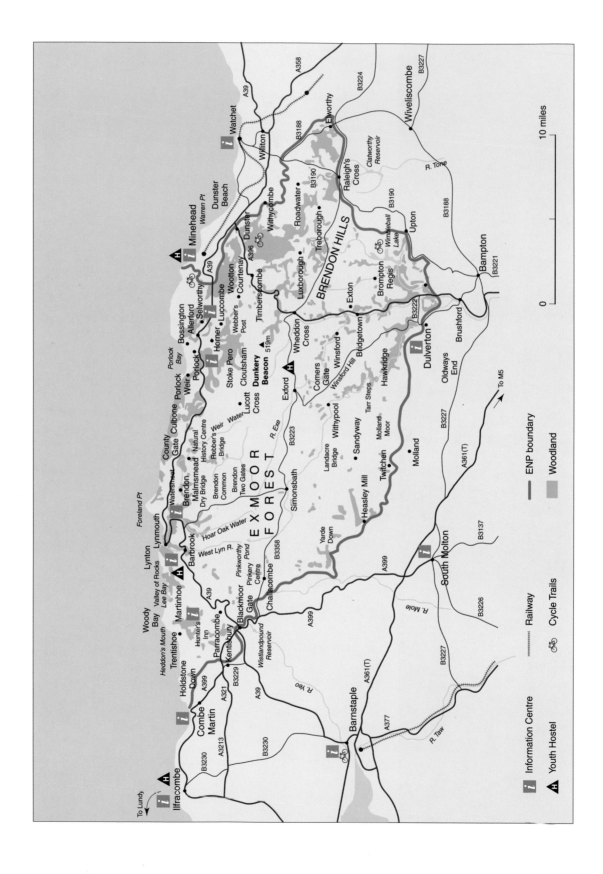

To Lundy

Ilfracombe

Combe Martin

Holdstone Down

Trentishoe

Martinhoe

Woody Bay

Lee Bay

Valley of Rocks

Heddon's Mouth

Hunter's Inn

Parracombe

Kentisbury

Lynton

Lynmouth

Foreland Pt

Barbrook

Blackmoor Gate

Challacombe

Pinkworthy

Pinkery Pond Centre

West Lyn R.

Hoar Oak Water

Watersmeet

County Gate

Culbone

Porlock Weir

Porlock

Porlock Bay

Bossington

Allerford

Selworthy

Brendon

Malmsmead Natural History Centre

Dry Bridge

Brendon Common

Brendon Two Gates

Robber's Weir Bridge

EXMOOR FOREST

Simonsbath

Yarde Down

Landacre Bridge

Withypool

Sandyway

Heasley Mill

Molland Moor

Twitchen

Molland

Wistlandpound Reservoir

R. Yeo

Barnstaple

R. Taw

R. Mole

South Molton

Oldways End

Brushford

Dulverton

Bampton

Upton

Wimbleball Lake

Hawkridge

Tarr Steps

Comers Gate

Winsford

Winsford Hill

Bridgetown

Exton

Brompton Regis

Wheddon Cross

Exford

Stoke Pero

Cloutsham

Dunkery Beacon 519m

Lucott Cross

Webber's Post

Horner

Luccombe

Wootton Courtenay

Timberscombe

Dunster

Withycombe

Roadwater

Treborough

Luxborough

BRENDON HILLS

Clatworthy Reservoir

Raleigh's Cross

R. Tone

Wiveliscombe

Elworthy

Williton

Watchet

Dunster Beach

Warren Pt

Minehead

Foreland Pt

Woodland

To M5

Information Centre

Youth Hostel

ENP boundary

Woodland

Railway

Cycle Trails

0   10 miles

A358
A39
B3224
B3227
B3188
B3190
B3190
B3188
B3221
A396
A39
A39
B3223
B3358
A399
A399
A39
A39
A361(T)
A377
A361(T)
B3226
B3227
B3137
B3230
B3229
A321
A3213
B3230
B3222
B3222
R. Exe

Foreword

by Professor Ian Mercer CBE, Secretary General, Association of National Park Authorities

The National Parks of Great Britain are very special places. Their landscapes include the most remote and dramatic hills and coasts in England and Wales, as well as the wild wetlands of the Broads. They still support the farming communities which have fashioned their detail over the centuries. They form the highest rank of the protected areas which society put in place in 1949. So, 1999 saw the fiftieth anniversary of the founding legislation which, incidentally, provided for Areas of Outstanding Natural Beauty, Nature Reserves, Areas of Special Scientific Interest and Long Distance Footpaths, as well as for National Parks.

In the eight years following that, ten Parks were designated. The Lake District, the Peak, Snowdonia and Dartmoor were already well visited, as were the North York Moors, Pembrokeshire Coast, Yorkshire Dales and Exmoor which quickly followed. The Brecon Beacons and Northumberland had their devotees too, though perhaps in lesser numbers then. The special quality of each of these places was already well known, and while those involved may not have predicted the numbers, mobility or aspirations of visitors accurately, the foresight of the landscape protection system cannot be too highly praised.

That system has had to evolve — not just to accommodate visitor numbers, but to meet the pressures flowing from agricultural change, hunger for housing and roadstone, thirst for water, and military manoeuvring — and indeed, the Norfolk and Suffolk Broads were added to the list in 1989. National Parks are now cared for by free-standing authorities who control development, hold land, grant-aid farmers and others, provide wardens, information, car parks and loos, clear footpaths and litter, plant trees and partner many other agents in pursuit of the purposes for which National Parks exist. Those purposes are paramount for all public agencies' consideration when they act within the Parks. They are:

- the conservation of the natural beauty, wildlife and cultural heritage of the area, and
- the promotion of the understanding and enjoyment of its special qualities by the public.

The National Park Authorities must, in pursuing those purposes, foster social and economic well-being. They now bring in some £48 million a year between them to be deployed in the Parks, in addition to normal local public spending.

This book is first a celebration of the National Park, of all its special qualities and of the people whose predecessors produced and maintained the detail of its character. The series to which this book belongs celebrates too the first fifty years of National Park protection in the United Kingdom, the foresight of the founding fathers, and the contributions since of individuals like John Sandford, Reg Hookway and Ron Edwards. The book and the series also mark the work of the present National Park Authorities and their staff, at the beginning of the next fifty years, and of the third millennium of historic time. Their dedication to their Parks is only matched by their aspiration for the sustainable enhancement of the living landscapes for which they are responsible. They need, and hope for, your support.

In the new century, national assets will only be properly maintained if the national will to conserve them is made manifest to national governments. I hope this book will whet your appetite for the National Park, or help you get more from your visit, and provoke you to use your democratic influence on its behalf. In any case it will remind you of the glories of one of the jewels in Britain's landscape crown. Do enjoy it.

Introducing Exmoor

Exmoor, as its name suggests, is the moor on which the River Exe rises. Beyond that it is not easy to give it rigid boundaries. It is essentially a high moorland plateau which falls away gradually at most edges, except to the north, where it drops abruptly and dramatically to the Bristol Channel. At the other edges fields have encroached, unfortunately making much of Exmoor ex-moor, and it cannot be defined by moorland alone.

The National Park boundary is definite but debate may still be possible about what should and should not have been included. The Countryside Agency's Exmoor Landscape Character Area extends to the Atlantic coast of North Devon, because of the common influence of Devonian rocks on the landscape. Original plans were for the Park to extend to the Quantocks, which has similar rocks and character. Although the Quantocks were considered a landscape of National Park quality, the area between them and Exmoor was not, and the Quantocks were con-sidered too small to be a separate National Park. It then became one of the country's first Areas of Outstanding Natural Beauty.

The National Park does, however, extend beyond the moorland plateau and includes the Brendon Hills, outlying ridges around Minehead and the Vale of Porlock. The whole covers 267sq miles (692sq km), about two thirds of which lies in West Somerset and one third in North Devon.

About 10,500 people live within the National Park boundary. Around half of these live in towns and villages and the other half in scattered hamlets, farmhouses and cottages. The main settlements are Lynton and Lynmouth, Dulverton, Porlock and Dunster. To most inhabitants of these fringe settlements, however, Exmoor is still somewhere 'upover'.

As with the area, it is difficult to define a distinct Exmoor community or cul-ture. The isolation of settlements has led to diversity rather than conformity. The countryside way of life is often seen as the common culture. There are current attempts to ally the local communities against threats to this and to make hunting

Above: Traditional thatched cottages at Dunster
Left: Coppiced oaks in Badgworthy Wood

an issue around which to make a stand. There are certainly more Exmoor people for hunting than against and it is a way of life for many, but there is no general agreement.

Farming is not the dominant industry it used to be, and many more people nowadays are employed in service industries, particularly tourism. Partly through the work of the National Park Authority, there is unity in marketing Exmoor as a tourist destination. The Authority does not promote Exmoor but works with tourist organisations to ensure that it is promoted in a way that satisfies National Park purposes. Ask local people what spoils Exmoor and commercialisation comes top of the list, along with the traffic, the clutter of signs, and tea shops instead of village shops.

Yet all is relative, and Exmoor is actually extremely quiet and unspoiled. In fact it could be argued that Exmoor is the quietest, least problematic and least spoilt of all the National Parks. A recent survey shows fewer visitors coming to Exmoor than any other National Park and a very small number actually staying within the Park boundaries. Those who do come, however, tend to come time and time again. To them Exmoor is a discovery, their very own special place.

SPECIAL PLACES
National Parks in England and Wales resulted from over a century of pressure on successive governments from conservation and amenity organisations. During World War II the Government asked civil servant John Dower to report on which areas would make suitable

National Parks and why. John Dower was also Secretary of the Standing Council for National Parks, a committee of members of amenity organisations pressing for National Parks. His report listed Exmoor as one of twelve potential areas.

In 1949 an Act of Parliament enabled the creation of National Parks in England and Wales. Areas which qualified had to be large areas of great natural beauty, with plenty of opportunity for open air recreation and within easy reach of centres of population. Ten areas, including Exmoor, became National Parks and the Broads were later given similar status under a separate act. Today we recognise that the whole of our countryside is valued and relatively accessible, but the National Parks still contain the greatest tracts of open countryside, the grandest and most dramatic scenery, and give the strongest sense of remoteness where nature seems to predominate.

However, National Parks in England and Wales are not wilderness areas. Their characteristic landscapes reflect the interaction between man and nature. A thriving and culturally distinct local population is essential to maintain character. As

Top: Coastal heath above Lynch Combe (courtesy National Trust)
Above: Snowdrops in the Avill valley
Left: Watersmeet from Chiselcombe (courtesy National Trust)
Pages 12-13: A toll road offers a gentler alternative to the notorious Porlock Hill

Top: The Exmoor plateau: the Exe valley from Prayway Head
Above: Characteristic buildings: Chimneys at Dulverton

urban life becomes more artificial and technologically driven, the value of our National Parks' special qualities of tranquillity, remoteness and wildness becomes greater. It is anticipated that visitors will seek forms of recreation compatible with these qualities: quiet activities; outdoor pursuits; spiritual refreshment and study.

The purposes of National Parks are:
• to conserve and enhance the natural beauty, wildlife and cultural heritage; and
• to promote opportunities for the understanding and enjoyment of their special qualities.

WHY EXMOOR?

Most of Exmoor is fields of pasture. Some say that it is the moorland that makes it special, but less than a quarter of the National Park is moor and heath. Some say that it is the wooded combes (small valleys), but these are much more characteristic of areas south of Exmoor. Others say it is the diversity of wildlife, but this is relatively low on the moorlands and uplands. However, without these natural and semi-natural features Exmoor would not be Exmoor and not worthy of National Park status.

The Government worked up John Dower's suggestions into specific proposals through the Hobhouse Committee in 1947. Its Report cited many reasons why Exmoor should be a National Park. Its natural beauty included: the fine heather, bracken and grass moorland; the plateau seamed with wooded combes; the beautifully wooded valleys of the Exe, Barle and Haddeo; the cliffs and woods along the coast; the red deer, half-wild Exmoor ponies, ravens, buzzards, peregrine falcons and botanical rarities. Its **unspoiled character** included: the fine views to Dartmoor and Wales; Iron Age and Roman fortifications; historic buildings at Dunster; fine and beautiful churches at Porlock and Selworthy; pack horse bridges; the rich pasture and arable land of the Vale of Porlock; the thatched cottages of Winsford and Selworthy. Its **potential for open air recreation** included: the many bridleways and tracks and good access; the network of country lanes suitable for cycling and walking; the unrivalled potential for and interest in riding; the fishing for trout and salmon on the Lyn, Exe and Barle; the literary associations.

THE CHARACTER OF THE LAND

So, Exmoor is special because it is a large tract of relatively wild and unspoiled countryside with plenty of open space providing scope for quiet outdoor recreation. As such it is unusual for southern England and, unsurprisingly perhaps, the majority of its visitors come from that area. However, there are other West Country moors and Dartmoor is half as big again. So what makes Exmoor different?

The answer from most people would be simply that it *feels* different. It is physically different from most moors of Devon and Cornwall in that it is not granite. The granite weathers into the familiar rocky outcrops known as tors, and the weathered material has slipped from around them to produce concave slopes. On Exmoor the slopes are smooth, rounded and convex and the rock is rarely exposed,

Below: The central moorland: the Barle valley at Cow Castle

Above: Lynton: a Conservation Area
Opposite: Coastal heath at
Cosgate Hill

except on the coast. The valleys feel smaller, more enclosed, more intimate. To some, Dartmoor is the male landscape and Exmoor the female. Blackmore described an Exmoor scene looking as if 'all the country had a woman's hand on it' and Exmoor country really feels like 'Mother Earth'. The weather can be rough at times but the landscape never feels bleak or intimidating. You might feel the possibility of becoming lost in it, but you would hardly mind doing so. For many it is the variety of scenery that appeals. Nothing seems endless except the variety: it always feels that there is something else of interest around the corner. Criss-crossed by so many small roads and tracks, on Exmoor it seems that there is always a different way between A and B and, on arrival, you are often left wondering how you got there!

Before the Romantic Movement, people saw the landscape in a utilitarian way. Early travellers described Exmoor in terms such as: 'a very sound sheep pasture'; 'yielding but a very poor kind of turf of little value' or 'a solitarie place it is, the more commodious for Staggs'. Daniel Defoe, a seventeenth-century visitor, said: 'The country is called Exmore, Cambden calls it a filthy, barren ground, and so it is.' Both were briefly passing through and warmed to Exmoor when they got to know the area better. William Camden later called it 'a master-piece of Nature, perform'd when she was in her best and gayest humour'. Exmoor seems to warm to people and they to it. Few who know it well do not have an affection for it, and the landscape seems to have something to offer for everyone.

THE CHARACTER OF BUILDINGS

The vernacular or local style of architecture which survives on Exmoor belongs to that of South Wales and the northern parts of Devon, Cornwall and Somerset. A common feature is the chimneys which were added to the façades of new or old houses from the late sixteenth to early eighteenth centuries. The older houses would originally have been 'hearth houses', with a fireplace in the centre of the main room and smoke escaping through the thatch. Chimneys became necessary when an upper storey was added in the roof space and the smoke could no longer travel straight out. Families would add fireplaces to their homes as they grew wealthier. It was simplest to build a fireplace into an outside wall, but here a tall chimney was needed to draw the smoke above the ridge of the roof and sparks away from the thatch. Such chimneys were proudly displayed as status symbols. The bulging bread ovens at their bases reflect the fact that the living rooms which they heated were also the kitchens.

Today Exmoor has a variety of building styles. Each settlement has its own special character. Those in the Vale of Porlock are the most homogenous, and at Timberscombe, most buildings are of red sandstone from the same quarry. Wootton Courtenay's high garden walls are unusual. Estate cottages are unique to the estate, such as John Crispin's designs for cottages around Chargot, which are similar to the well-known cottages at Milton Abbas in Dorset. Their distinctive bulging façades have earned the local nickname of the 'pregnant cottages'. Designs by John Nash and Charles Voysey were

Above: Upland and lowland heaths merge: Lucott Moor and Dunkery Hill (courtesy National Trust)

adapted to suit local materials on the Holnicote and Ashley Combe estates.

What is unique about many Exmoor settlements, however, is not individual building styles but the settings and combinations of buildings. This is why the historic cores of eleven Exmoor towns and villages and five smaller settlements have been selected as Conservation Areas, where all the features which make up their character are conserved.

Lynton has a typical Conservation Area. The town grew in a wonderful natural setting in a valley shared with the Valley of Rocks. Its oldest buildings tend to be listed as being of Architectural or Historic Interest, but most of the character of the town is created by later building in the quirky, mixed styles of late Victorian times. There is, however, harmony created by the use of local stone and terracotta tiles and the prevalence of Swiss-style architecture. Lynton sold itself to tourists as the 'English Switzerland' and many buildings have front-facing gables with ornately carved barge boards and balconies like those in the Alps.

TRAVELLING TO EXMOOR

There are few day trippers to Exmoor except those staying in surrounding tourist resorts, and most visitors stay a while when they are in the area. The size of Exmoor might suggest that it can be 'done' in a day, but a lifetime can be spent exploring it without feeling that you have 'done' it yet. So do not underestimate the time it takes to move around Exmoor or rush a visit.

Most people arrive by car and from the east, so the M4 and M5 are preferred routes, although from London the M3 and A303 are as fast and more direct. Those travelling to West Somerset tend to exit the M5 at Bridgwater or Taunton and those for North Devon take the A361 'link road' via Tiverton. The A39 coast road is much more scenic but has three of the country's most notorious hills: Porlock, Countisbury and Lynmouth, within a 10-mile stretch, and these are best avoided with a caravan. Once on Exmoor, the roads are not congested, but there are only two A-class roads traversing the National Park and they are slow and winding. But then, that is part of the charm. So you could really enjoy driving on Exmoor but, if you are not used to constant changing of gears, not certain of the width of your car and not used to reversing long distances on narrow, winding roads, you might not.

The soundest advice is not to try to 'do' Exmoor by car. Running about in vehicles sightseeing is not what National Parks were intended for and is not very environment friendly. Spend a while exploring a small area at a time. If you do not indulge in the 'green' forms of locomotion such as walking, cycling or horse-riding, public transport is a viable alternative. As much of the population and tourist activity is along the coast, that is the area best supplied with public transport and the most convenient area to stay if you do not have a car. Trains run from Exeter to Barnstaple along what is known as the 'Tarka Line', and from Taunton to Minehead via a short bus link along the privately run West Somerset Railway and several buses run outwards from those destinations.

Along the coast, the main tourist season tends to be the traditional ten weeks of English summer. Inland, however, the 'shoulders' of the season in spring and autumn are often busier, as many come for the country sports or simply to avoid the perceived busy time. Late August and early September is the time to see the heather in bloom, but each season has its pleasures. May and June used to be the driest months but, in these days of climatic change, the dry months are getting earlier, the winters milder and the summers wetter. Whenever you come, you need to prepare for any weather. However, for an upland area, Exmoor is unusually mild and that is one of its many attractions.

Below left: One of Dunster's many tea shops
Below: Rhododendron invades coastal heath above Countisbury Cove (courtesy National Trust)

1 The rocks beneath: geology and scenery

Exmoor's landscape is unique. Its plateau, its smoothly rounded, convexly curving hillsides and deep little combes are quite distinctive and unlike any other upland in Britain, apart from the neighbouring Quantocks.

This is partly due to sedimentary rocks and the effects on them of frost activity during the Ice Age. The Ice Age was not a continuous period of cold, but one of fluctuating climate and sea levels. Exmoor's sea cliffs, the highest in England, are of a 'hog's-back' shape which reflects these changes. Perhaps the best examples are the Hangman Hills. Their gentler upper cliff slopes were shaped under icy conditions while the hills were stranded far inland by dropping sea levels. The vertical lower parts of the cliffs show marine erosion caused by rises in sea level in periods of warm climate. Exmoor's hog's-backed cliffs are best viewed from a distance, such as from Bossington Hill and from the South West Coast Path to the west of Combe Martin.

THE ROCKS

Rocks of an age first studied in Devon have given their name to the Devonian period of time, which lasted from about 410 million years ago to 360 million years ago. Exmoor's rocks show a remarkably complete record of this period and its transition with the following Carboniferous period – a record which is fragmentary elsewhere in the world.

Above: Long Chains Combe: a valley shaped by Ice Age weathering
Left: Ashton Cleave: screes from Ice Age frosts cover many Exmoor valley sides

EXMOOR'S SAHARA

In the red rocks we find sediments which represent all the elements of a desert landscape: the sands of sand dunes and shorelines, the breccias (broken rocks) of scree slopes, the muds of dried-up lakes and river beds, and conglomerates, which are mixtures of pebbles and silt from flash floods descending from the mountains. Cliffs at Glenthorne have been designated a Site of Special Scientific Interest because they show a variety of these features.

Above: Fossils of the sea shell Myalina *at Wild Pear Beach*
Right: Tufa: a natural concrete at Wild Pear Beach
Opposite: Terminal curvature: shales at Challacombe folded by Ice Age soil movements

At that time the world was almost unrecognisable from that of today and the area where the future rocks of Exmoor were forming was south of the Equator. This was on the southern edge of a mountainous continent which consisted of today's North America and Northern Europe joined together. Proof of this is provided by the fact that rocks continuous with those of Exmoor's are now found in Greenland.

The Devonian period is part of the Palaeozoic era, which means the time when life was just beginning on Earth. It was well before the age of dinosaurs, and there was little life on land at the time. Not surprisingly, there are few fossils in Exmoor's coarser sediments, which were laid down on land. Iron is a common constituent of rocks and the red colour of the Exmoor sandstones is due to hematite, an iron oxide. Today's wet Exmoor climate would react with the iron to form rust-coloured hydroxides but the redness is evidence of an arid climate. Exmoor's rocks are called 'sedimentary' because they were formed as sediments in rivers, in the sea or on land as desert sands. They vary according to the size of sediment: mud has formed shales, sand has formed sandstones and larger particles have formed grits, conglomerates and breccias.

The Devonian rocks are best exposed along the coast. They are most accessible in the Valley of Rocks where, if you look carefully, you can find a variety of shales, sandstones and limestones with a few fossils. At Combe Martin beach there are younger Devonian rocks of equal variety and at Heddon's Mouth beach you can see the transition between the grey-coloured marine sediments of the Lower Devonian and the red desert sandstones of the Middle Devonian. Interesting structures can be seen in the cliffs at Glenthorne and Greenaleigh, but this requires some steep walking.

Some of Exmoor's sediments were, however, laid down in the sea or in the mouths of rivers, and fossilised shells and skeletons of sea creatures, including some of the earliest fish, have been found. Exmoor's limestones represent former

coral reefs – showing that the seas in which they were formed were tropical. Thin bands of limestone are found at Combe Martin and in the Brendon Hills, where they have been quarried to make lime for cement, plaster or neutralising the acidity of moorland soils. At Combe Martin springs from the limestone have deposited lime over rocks fallen from the cliffs, forming a natural concrete known as tufa. Here also is a hard band of limestone stained purple with iron minerals. In places it has been weathered to leave the brown mineral, umber, which has been quarried for pigment. Pebbles from this hard limestone are washed far along Exmoor's coast before they are worn down and are easily recognisable because they contain fossilised fragments of crinoids – colonies of creatures known as 'sea lilies'.

Colliding continents created folds which become more acute towards the point of collision to the south west of Exmoor. In the finer sediments, such structures can be seen on an even smaller scale, helping us to understand processes which elsewhere can only be examined in parts over a wide area. The pressures of earth movements had different effects according to the type of sediment. The coarser sediments tended to stay in 'massive' beds, whereas thin bands of limestone buckled like plastic and the mud which had compressed to form shale sheared into flat pieces along lines known as 'slaty cleavage'. In places they formed slates which have been used locally for roofing material. Such rocks are known as 'metamorphic', meaning that they have been changed greatly from the original sediments. Many Exmoor rocks are a sort of half-way house, where they show slaty cleavage but are still recognisable as the original sediments.

THE LANDSCAPE

As well as being folded, Exmoor's rocks have been moved along cracks known as faults. These were created by those Carboniferous earth movements and by much later ones which also built the Alps. One of the older faults was caused by the Dunkery area rising relative to land to the north. In the desert climate, flash floods

DRIFTING CONTINENTS

Most Exmoor sediments have been changed by great pressures from earth movements which lifted them out of the sea during the Carboniferous period, about 300 million years ago. Continental drift caused a continent roughly comprising today's Africa and South America to collide with the northern continent, squashing Exmoor's rocks in between. Most of what is now the area between South Devon and South Wales was folded like a concertina. Exmoor ended up on a ridge known as an anticline and the once-horizontal strata, or layers of rock, now rest at angles, mostly dipping towards the south, although some roll over the crest of the ridge and run down towards the Bristol Channel.

VIEWING THE PLATEAU

Good impressions of the Exmoor plateau can be obtained from walks into the wild grass moors of The Chains above Pinkery or to Larkbarrow from Larkbarrow Gate, while good views of the Vale of Porlock can be had from Selworthy and Crawter Hill above Porlock. Perhaps the most spectacular view of the Vale is from the path around the flank of Bossington Hill, from where the former coastline around Porlock is clearly illustrated.

Opposite: Folding of sandstones at Combe Martin weir
Below: A rejuvenated valley: Heddon Valley at Hunter's Inn (courtesy National Trust)

worked their way along the fault to form a valley. Temporary lakes formed in the valley, leaving muddy sediments as they dried up. Then followed a relatively quiet 100 million years when the hills were worn down to a plain. Fragments of rock ran down into the valley as screes, later to form New Red Sandstones, named because they were reworked from the old ones. New Red Sandstones can be seen in the Vale of Porlock, and an interesting exposure can be seen in the side of a lane at Ordnance Survey GR SS912451, a short walk from Luccombe.

Eventually, the sea rose and the valley was flooded. Marine sediments from this period – the Jurassic – are found around Selworthy and Minehead. We do not know the extent of the flooding, but the chances are that by the following period – the Cretaceous – the whole of Exmoor was submerged. Within another 100 million years, the area had been lifted back out of the sea by those Alpine earth movements. The current theory is that it was lifted as a block, known as a 'horst' block, separated from surrounding rocks by many faults. In the process it was slightly tilted towards the south and east. At Combe Martin is a large fault where Exmoor seems to have been lifted about 500ft (150m) above the area to the west and the Exmoor cliffs stand proud of younger rocks in the Bristol Channel, which you would expect to lie above them. Where there were any younger sediments on top of Exmoor, they have since been eroded. Protected by sea or sediment, the drowned plain was exhumed as the Exmoor plateau, and that ancient desert valley as the Vale of Porlock. These are far older than most features of the Earth's surface, including the main mountain ranges and the continents themselves.

Such features have survived the erosion of ice which affected most of Britain, and Exmoor's landscape shows an exceptionally long history. The plateau is stepped around the edges, a feature well illustrated at Molland Moor. Some say that this is due to phases of erosion as Exmoor rose out of the sea over the last 50 million years, while some of the steps are clearly due to faulting.

Exmoor valleys show how rivers have cut down in stages as sea level has dropped, stood still and dropped again. An unusual feature is where valleys widen, narrow and widen again along their course. The narrowing is known as 'rejuvenation' and is where the river has started to cut down again in response to a drop in sea level. The distinctiveness of many of Exmoor's steep-sided combes is due to this. Also unusual are the knolls on the floors and sides of valleys. These show where rivers meandered over flood plains cut before rejuvenation. The best-known knolls are at Flexbarrow and Cow Castle, which can be found by walking along the River Barle south of Simonsbath. A valley side knoll from the same terrace can also be seen at Kingsland Pits, further downstream.

Some Exmoor streams have not been able to cut their valleys down as fast as the rising sea has worn back the coast. As a result, coastal waterfalls cascade down the cliffs; a rare feature worldwide and more typical of Norwegian fjords. Conversely, when sea levels dropped in

the colder parts of the Ice Age, Exmoor rivers cut rapidly back from the coast, leaving remarkably deep gorges such as that of the East Lyn.

The best views of coastal waterfalls can be had from the sea, with regular boat trips running from Lynmouth and Ilfracombe in the summer. A steep walk to the beach at Woody Bay will be rewarded by a view of the fall of Hanging Water, and along the spectacular stretch of the South West Coast Path between Woody Bay and the Heddon Valley, Hollow Brook Fall is crossed.

PORLOCK SHINGLE RIDGE

Across Porlock Bay lies one of Britain's best examples of a 'baymouth bar'. It is formed by the process of 'longshore drift', whereby shingle is moved eastwards along the coast by waves backed by westerly winds. The shingle is replaced by fresh material from cliff falls further west. Most is of cobble size but smaller, pebble-sized shingle survives at the less exposed eastern end of the bay. As sea levels have risen the ridge has moved inland. It once formed a spit, leaving the bay open at the eastern end. It then formed a bar, closing the bay.

It has covered a woodland which grew on the marsh between 7,800 and 5,000 years ago. Tree stumps and peat are exposed on the shore at low tide and known as the 'submarine forest'. There is also evidence from the peat of Mesolithic people and aurochs (wild oxen) living there at the same time. The submarine forest is accessible from Porlock Weir at low tide but requires some difficult walking across cobbles. It can be found at Ordnance Survey GR SS871478.

Despite occasional breaches by winter storms, the lake formed behind the ridge was gradually drained for grazing marshes. Groynes were built along the beach to protect the ridge. Recent storms have, however, caused the sea to breach the ridge and form a tidal lagoon on the marsh. A theory is that the groynes caused the ridge to steepen and make it less stable. Many now feel that it is best not to interfere and let Nature take its course.

Above left: Coastal waterfall at Sir Robert's Chair
Above: Porlock shingle ridge
Opposite: 'Submarine forest' in Porlock Bay
Pages 28-9: The coastline west of North Walk, Lynton, showing erosion of Exmoor's 'hog's back' cliffs

Exmoor mining has had a long, if sporadic, history but the National Park is unusual in Britain in having no active mines or quarries. The last iron mines were worked in World War I but prospecting for iron, copper, uranium and even gold continued throughout the twentieth century and reserves await the right economic conditions for exploitation. A vein of iron ore known as the Roman Lode appears to run across Exmoor from the Brendon Hills to Simonsbath and beyond, and recent research has shown that iron smelting on Exmoor goes back at least to Roman times. Eisen, the German word for iron, was given to a hill near Winsford by German miners who worked there in the sixteenth century. At that time, the copper mines at Molland were the most productive in the world. The heyday of Exmoor iron mining was, however, the late ninteenth century, when Exmoor mines supplied ore to the booming iron and steel industry in South Wales.

The remains of Exmoor's mine buildings are unusual in their rural settings and style. The adits of iron mines in the seaward faces of Great and Little Hangman can hardly be more spectacular in their setting. Here ore was dumped over the cliff to be picked up by small boats from the treacherous shore below, a process which eventually proved too dangerous for the survival of the sailors or the mines. In days when Exmoor roads were not suited to wheeled traffic, transport often added prohibitively to the cost of ore which was already expensive to extract. Running from Simonsbath towards Porlock Weir can be traced the bed of a mineral railway started by Frederic Knight but never finished, because his ore proved not valuable enough to warrant the expense. More successful was the mineral railway connecting iron mines along the ridge of the Brendon Hills. This was in turn connected to a line to the port of Watchet via a steep incline which ran from near Ralegh's Cross. Laden trucks ran down the incline by gravity and empty trucks were winched back up by a steam engine set below the track at the top. The remains of the incline and its engine house are now owned by the National Park Authority and can still be seen, as can Exmoor's last remaining mine engine house at nearby Burrow Farm.

Today, mineral veins are mostly found outcropping along inaccessible parts of the coast and old mines and spoil heaps are mostly out of bounds to the public. At the northern end of Combe Martin beach, however, can be found an iron vein, strings of quartz, and old trial adit for silver and traces of silver-bearing galena, which can also be found at the northern end of Wild Pear Beach.

Opposite: Ripple-marked sandstones in the Valley of Rocks
Below: Remains of the Brendon Hills iron mining: Burrow Farm engine house

2 Climate, vegetation and wildlife

Above: Badgworthy Water in winter
Opposite above: Sea mist shrouds
Countisbury Hill (courtesy National
Trust)
Opposite below: A rare drought at
Wimbleball Lake

The West Country is generally thought of as having a milder climate than the rest of Britain, because it is further south and more influenced by the sea. Most weather recording sites in the region are around the coast and resorts vie with one another over claims for record summer temperatures and length of sunshine.

Up on the moors, of course, it is a different story. It can be said of Exmoor that its climate is relatively mild for a British upland, but it is an extremely varied area with an equally varied climate. Temperature naturally varies with altitude. On a journey from Dulverton to the coast there is normally a drop of 5°C by Winsford Hill, a mile out of the Barle valley. It may then drop another couple of degrees on the high ground above Simonsbath but within about three miles of the coast it returns to the temperature of Dulverton, even at the altitude of Winsford Hill, and warms even further by the time you reach the coast at Lynmouth.

Average temperatures for Exmoor range from about 15°C (59°F) in August to about 5°C (41°F) in February. The extremes tend to come in the more sheltered

areas and it is common to have frost at night in the valleys and milder conditions on the hills.

As with the rest of Britain, the climate of Exmoor is influenced by the prevailing south-westerly winds, which bring moist air off the Atlantic, and the Gulf Stream drift, which brings a milder climate than you would expect for the latitude. Some people predict that global warming will cause the current to move and bring a much colder climate to Britain. At present it rarely snows within about 3 miles of the coast and coastal hills can be snow-free while snow is lying on much lower ground inland. Nowadays, however, there is little snowfall at all, and since the late 1970s, winters have been much milder than before. It is common to see normally dormant animals such as bats and badgers active throughout the winter, and spring flowers such as snowdrops and primroses can be found in bloom from November onwards. Exmoor is now well within the range of birds which once had a much more southerly distribution, such as Dartford warblers, and it is normal to see little egrets and hoopoes throughout the summer.

Pages 36-7: Trees lean with prevailing winds on the Forest Wall at Broad Mead

The prevailing winds also bring precipitation, so that the south-western edge of the moor has the highest rainfall and snowfall. People who have lived on the moor all of their lives tend to head north east to retire in the rain shadow of Exmoor. Around Minehead and Porlock rainfall is about 35in (900mm) per annum whereas on the Exmoor plateau it is twice that amount, rising to 80in (2,030mm) on The Chains and Five Barrows. The greatest change is between Dunkery and the Vale of Porlock, where the rainfall drops by half in as little as 2 miles. As one might expect, such parts exposed to the north and north east have winds prevailing from that direction, particularly in summer months.

The driest months have traditionally been May and June. As the sea warms up, the summers become beset with mists and drizzle. Dunkery is often used as the weatherglass and it is said, 'When Dunkery's top cannot be seen, Horner will have a flooded stream.' The Lynmouth flood disaster of 1952 happened in summer, with heavy rain on an already wet moor, and flooding is becoming more frequent. Very occasionally, the rain is so heavy that it stands on the moor like a vast lake and runs as one continuous sheet rather than as rivers. The effect is bewildering and has to be seen to be believed.

Locals have plenty of sayings about rain. On the coast they say: 'If you can see Wales it is going to rain; if you can't it is already raining.' The saying has some truth in that there is often a temporary ridge of high pressure over the Bristol Channel with depressions on either side. Global warming is producing more rain – some say in the summer, some in the winter. The drier months seem to be becoming earlier and Easter is becoming busier with tourists. So, the advice is come early and come prepared. It certainly does not rain all of the time and when it does it is usually 'soft' rain. When it is not 'soft' it is, as one writer described it, 'as bracing as a showerbath; as exhilarating as champagne', so who cares?

VARIETY IS THE SPICE OF LIFE

As climate varies, so do habitats, and Exmoor is a place where the ranges of creatures with contrasting needs overlap. In common with other upland areas it does not have a great diversity of wildlife, although it is as great in the Vale of Porlock as anywhere in Somerset. Biodiversity, which means the variety of wildlife, is one of the main aims of conservation.

Below: Horner Woods National Nature Reserve (courtesy National Trust)

Exmoor has Britain's greatest extent of broadleaved coastal woodland and much of its woodland is relatively undisturbed ancient woodland – about as close to our natural vegetation as we come in England, and which supports our greatest diversity of wildlife. Other habitats, although supporting a smaller variety of species, are important contributors to biodiversity on an international scale. A large proportion of Britain's lichen species can be found on Exmoor. Well over a thousand species of moths have been found and many species of insects are added to the Exmoor list annually. Several species of birds of prey can be seen, including buzzard, merlin, hobby, peregrine, kestrel, sparrowhawk and, in winter, red kite, hen harrier and goshawk.

The flora of Exmoor has much in common with other parts of Europe's Atlantic seaboard. The distribution of some of its plants is described as 'lusitanian', after an old name for Portugal, where similar plants may be found. For instance, *Pinguicula lusitanica*, a rare butterwort, is an insect-eating plant found from Portugal to Exmoor. Much of Exmoor's characteristic vegetation – its heathland and its sessile oakwoods – is also characteristic of this part of Europe. Sessile means 'without a stalk,' and the sessile oak is a small variety of oak with acorns and flowers which appear stalkless.

Moor and heath are both semi-natural habitats. They are natural in the sense that the plants which live there are naturally occurring and not introduced or planted, but man-made in the sense that man has excluded the trees which would normally grow in such locations. In the absence of grazing by farm animals and deliberate burning, scrub then woodland would take over. In true wilderness, this 'natural succession' can be seen across the edges of habitats as well as through time.

On Exmoor there are relatively wild places where you can follow the succession by walking from heath through scrub to scattered birch and pine trees into thick oak woodland. Such transitional areas are among the most diverse and important areas for wildlife but are rarely allowed to develop because of the way in which man creates artificial boundaries between habitats.

PLANTS ON TREES

Visitors from elsewhere are often impressed by plants growing on trees, such as polypody ferns and bearded lichen, and the flowers of banks and walls, such as the purple foxglove, rock stonecrop, wall pennywort, pellitory-of-the-wall and ferns like the maidenhair spleenwort. Exmoor is one of the main places in Britain to find Irish spurge and Cornish moneywort, flowers which like shady stream banks, and ivy-leaved bellflower, a small, blue-flowered plant growing on bogs. June is probably the best month to see these plants in flower.

Top: Pale butterwort in the Barle valley
Above: Sessile oaks in the East Lyn valley (courtesy National Trust)

SPECIAL SITES

The significance of rare habitats on Exmoor has been recognised in the designation of Sites of Special Scientific Interest (SSSIs) and the National Nature Reserve at Horner. Exmoor's biggest SSSI, known as North Exmoor, shows successions from ancient semi-natural woodland through upland heath to blanket bog. The South Exmoor and Exmoor Coastal Heaths SSSIs show transitions from lowland to upland heath and coastal heath to maritime grassland.

Above: Blanket bog on Broad Mead
Right: Bracken on heathland at Lucott Moor (courtesy National Trust)
Opposite top left: Oakwoods descend to the sea at Embelle
Opposite top right: Winter drifts of purple moor grass at Brendon Two Gates
Opposite centre: Stonechat on Winsford Hill
Opposite below: Mating heath fritillaries on Dunkery

RARE HABITATS

Roughly a third of the National Park is covered with semi-natural vegetation. Nowhere on Exmoor is unaffected by the impact of man, but in these areas plants which occur naturally and have not been planted are in the majority. If Exmoor were wilderness most of it would be covered with a mixture of broadleaved woodland trees. The closest you can get to nature now is on the shore and some of the sea cliffs, where mixed woodland survives out of reach of fire or grazing sheep, or where it is too exposed for trees and heath or grassland occurs naturally.

Exmoor has been farmed for at least 5,000 years and the most potent force in the removal of tree cover has been grazing farm animals – in particular, sheep. Through their grazing of young trees they have prevented woodlands from regenerating. Deforestation, rain washing nutrients from the soil, and continual grazing and swaling (deliberate burning) has suited the growth of moor and heath.

These terms cover a great variety of types of open, low-growing vegetation and are largely defined by their types of soil. Both have acid, peaty soils, but moor is on waterlogged soils and heath on freely-drained soils. Even in high rainfall areas, heath vegetation is well adapted for drought. A greater depth of peat develops on moor. Peat is the accumulation of dead plant material which forms where acidity and waterlogging of the soil inhibits the organisms which normally cause it to decay.

Moorland develops in wet and cool, yet equable climates such as on Europe's Atlantic coast. It may seem common in the British Isles, but it is internationally rare and Britain has up to 15 per cent of the world's total. Exmoor's moors are predominantly grassland supporting few species. However, one type, consisting mostly of purple moor grass and meadow thistle, is unusual. Britain also has a large percentage of the world's upland and western heaths, of which Exmoor has significant quantities. Some types of heath on Exmoor are only found in South Wales and the West Country and one type, dominated by bristle bent grass and western gorse, is particularly rare.

Another rare Exmoor habitat is woodland where ash and rowan predominate,

but it is the western oakwoods for which Exmoor is most important internationally. These tend to be dominated by small, crooked sessile oaks which have largely survived grazing through their past management for timber, bark and charcoal and present management for conservation. Naturally they would have a greater mixture of tree types but with the survival of tree cover for hundreds, if not thousands, of years has come the survival of many smaller plants. The same is true of the ancient trees in Exmoor's parklands, and Exmoor is of great importance for the variety of lichens, bryophytes and fungi associated with such trees which also occur in all of its semi-natural habitats. A large proportion of Britain's lichen species is found on Exmoor and some species are not found anywhere else.

CHARACTERISTIC SPECIES

Exmoor is noted as a stronghold for the dormouse. This charming creature is rarely seen as it is largely nocturnal and hibernates in winter. Its habitat is broadleaved woodland which usually includes an understorey of hazel. The ancient woods of the Barle valley between Withypool and Dulverton are particularly favoured by them.

Buzzards are as numerous here as anywhere in Britain and there is more than one breeding pair for every square mile of Exmoor. They are birds of the west of Britain, but this distribution is largely due to persecution elsewhere. They vary greatly in plumage and local birds are often almost white underneath, leading some to think they have seen ospreys (which do pass through Exmoor on migration).

WHINCHAT COUNTRY
Exmoor may have the country's largest concentration of whinchats. These summer visitors like Exmoor's heaths, scrub and partly-wooded valleys. Their close relative, the stonechat, is resident on Exmoor throughout the year and requires a similar habitat. The males can often be heard 'chatting' and 'wheeting' from the topmost spray of gorse or bramble. Many die in hard winters, and their requirement for heathland and a mild climate means that Exmoor is a national stronghold for these birds, especially near the coast.

Exmoor is the national bastion of what is possibly Britain's rarest breeding butterfly, the heath fritillary. Fritillaries are named after the Latin name for checkers and have brown and orange checks on the upper parts of their wings. The caterpillars of heath fritillaries feed on common cow wheat, a plant of woodland edges and clearings, and the colonies of butterflies

Above: Ancient oak pollards at East Water (courtesy National Trust)

tend to move around as new habitat becomes available. The adults can be seen in late June and July on heathland, especially near woods. Good places to look are in Doone Country, to the south of Malmsmead, and around the flanks of Dunkery Hill. Another rare fritillary, the high brown, also favours Exmoor. This prefers to spend its time in woodland glades, particularly where thistles grow, although its caterpillars feed on dog violet.

CONSERVATION

Although one of the functions of National Park Authorities is wildlife conservation, many people are surprised to find that National Parks are not nature reserves. Exmoor contains nature reserves, but wildlife has no additional legal protection here because it is in a National Park. Indeed, there is much hunting and shooting on Exmoor. This can help maintain habitats and if it were not for hunting interests, much of Exmoor's open country and woodlands would not have survived.

Like the rest of Britain, Exmoor has suffered greatly from loss of natural and semi-natural habitats. It lost an estimated 58 per cent of its ancient woodland from 1840 to 1979; 92 per cent of its unimproved grassland from 1930 to 1990; and 65 per cent of its moor and heath from 1913 to 1969. Much of the work of the National Park Authority is concentrated on protecting the remaining and now rare habitats, and the Authority has drawn up a map of those areas it considers most important to protect. Through English Nature, 27 per cent of Exmoor's moorland, woodland and coast are protected as Sites of Special Scientific Interest, which include our most important wildlife sites.

Much recent habitat loss has been due to subsidised agricultural improvements,

although this trend has been greatly reduced by new subsidies for conservation measures. Unfortunately, such schemes tend to be short lived and fluctuate with economics and politics. A switch to increased food production could easily reverse the effects of conservation measures.

A more effective method of ensuring habitat protection is through land ownership. Together the National Trust and the National Park Authority, with their similar aims of conservation and amenity, own over 17 per cent of the National Park. Other public landowners, such as the Forestry Commission, Crown Estate and Water Companies, own land for different purposes but have accords with the National Park Authority on conservation and amenity measures. However, protection from such organisations is not guaranteed to last forever, and 75 per cent of Exmoor still remains in private ownership. Ultimately, the conservation of Exmoor depends on the concern of individuals and the priority we all give it.

RED DEER

Exmoor is famous for its wild red deer, and the stag's head was a natural choice for the National Park's logo. It has England's largest concentration of these creatures and is the only part where they have remained continuously in the wild. Elsewhere they have been re-introduced or kept in parks. Once widely persecuted as a pest, they managed to survive on Exmoor through their protection as royal game in Exmoor Forest. When the Forest shrank in the thirteenth century, their main habitat in the wooded combes to the east of the moor was excluded and few survived. In the early nineteenth century, the havoc the deer caused to the expansion of corn and root crops resulted in their near extermination, with numbers down to

Above: Swaling: a controlled burn by National Park rangers on North Hill
Page 44: Red deer stags (Mark Thole)

WHERE TO SEE DEER
Red deer can be found all over Exmoor but tend to be most frequent around the wooded valleys of the Exe, Barle and Horner Water. Don't be surprised to see them grazing in fields, where they are often mistaken for farm animals. They are most active, and thus most noticeable, early and late in the day.

about 60. However, one or two concerned landowners gave protection and now they have spread to the edges of Cornwall and Dartmoor and to the Quantocks.

Annual counts suggest steady numbers of about 2,700 within the National Park. About 500 a year are culled by licence and about 100 or more are taken by the stag hunts. But the numbers taken by farmers and poachers must be at least as many again and to sustain such losses the population is likely to be higher than estimated. It is argued that the deer are tolerated because of the sport they provide and that they would be exterminated should hunting be banned. No doubt the numbers would decrease, but the deer range far beyond the hunting areas and there are numerous sanctuaries.

EXMOOR PONIES

Exmoor ponies are the nearest Britain has to truly wild horses and, arguably, one of the world's original races, from which all other horses are descended. Similar ponies roamed throughout the Northern Hemisphere during the Ice Age and adapted to life on the open steppes and plains with their harsh winters. Their double-layered coat is so effectively insulating that snow covers the ponies without melting. It is also good at shedding rain. The head is large and warms cold air before it reaches the lungs, and the 'toad' eyelids protect eyes from the elements. Exmoor ponies also have large lower jaws and thick lips to cope with tough vegetation, even gorse. In recent years, they have proved their worth as 'conservation grazers', keeping down unwanted scrub.

PONY GENE POOL

Today there are only a few hundred Exmoor ponies worldwide, and the handful of free-roaming ponies on Exmoor's moorland are crucial to the survival of the natural characteristics of the race. Wild they may be, but they are all carefully managed by their owners and selected through the specifications of the Exmoor Pony Society. For breeders, they are important to retain as a 'gene pool' of natural characteristics such as stamina and disease resistance, which can be passed on to other horses.

Below: Annual pony round-up on Haddon Hill

Exmoor ponies can be seen all over Exmoor. Although not all ponies on Exmoor are Exmoor ponies, most on the open moors are pure-bred, unlike those on Dartmoor. Their colouring is shades of brown, with no white markings. The best known herd, the Anchor herd, can be found on Winsford Hill. The National Park Authority has herds running on Haddon Hill, which overlooks Wimbleball Lake, and on its Exmoor Forest estate at Larkbarrow and Warren. Other good places to look include Porlock and Withypool Commons.

WHITEBEAMS

Seven different species of whitebeam trees grow on Exmoor. They are related to rowan but have larger berries and single leaves which are silvery underneath, hence the name. The berries are edible and were once sold in local markets under the name of 'French hales.' There are eleven British species in all, some of which are among the country's rarest trees, with only a handful of individuals. Three basic species have hybridised to form new species which are often very localised in their distribution. Because of their isolation, these have evolved a way of setting seed without fertilisation and effectively clone themselves.

Exmoor has three species of whitebeam which are endemic (ie found nowhere else) and is a stronghold for two other species which are confined to the West Country and South Wales. The endemic species are the slender whitebeam (*Sorbus sub-cuneata*), growing on the eastern coast; *Sorbus vexans*, growing on the central and western coast; and *Sorbus taxon D*, named after Desolate and Dogsworthy Combe on the central coast where it is found. These all prefer the less acid coastal soils. The pale undersides of their leaves are easily distinguished when looking up from the base of Exmoor cliffs. The other species are found mainly on the coast but are also seen around the East Lyn valley at Watersmeet and inland as far as Dulverton.

The Devon whitebeam (*Sorbus devoniensis*) is probably the easiest to identify, with brown berries and lacking the silvery leaves. You will need to have a very detailed guide to identify the other species. Even then identification may be difficult when they are not in flower, and that is most of the time.

Right: Sorbus vexans - *whitebeam - at Woody Bay*
Opposite: Woodland conservation: *heavy horses extract timber in Hawkcombe Woods*

3 Man's influence

Above: The Whitstones: Bronze Age standing stones on Porlock Common

Exmoor can be regarded as a largely untapped resource for the archaeologist. There is much supposition about many of Exmoor's archaeological features, but little hard evidence and expert investigation is still needed. Exmoor's history is remarkable in that there is so much to be discovered and so much to learn. However, while sites elsewhere are rapidly being destroyed by development or changes in land use, the pace of change on Exmoor is less noticeable, and its known historic sites are becoming more significant.

There are archaeological sites and monuments on Exmoor dating from all periods since the Stone Age. These range from Bronze Age barrows and Iron Age forts through Saxon and medieval settlements to more recent industrial remains. Recent important discoveries have included an Iron Age hill fort near Timberscombe and traces of iron smelting from the same period.

Exmoor's prehistoric stone rows are mainly of a type also found in South Wales but its stone settings are an example of local distinctiveness and few examples have been found elsewhere. They consist of groups of upright stones, usually quite small and often only visible after moorland fires. There are often groups of six or eight, arranged in geometric shapes such as rectangles or triangles or a combination of both. Often there are missing or buried stones so that the original shape is lost.

They are found mostly in the western half of the National Park and the best known are those in the former Royal Forest at Little Tom's Hill and East Pinford, where there are six stones in parallel rows of three, and Trout Hill, where there are four in a square. Some say that they are short stone rows or fragments of larger rows and that they date from the Bronze Age, but such rows are usually associated with barrows and mostly these are not. They could have had a religious or astronomical significance, but we know nothing about what they were for or their age and there is much scope for research.

SETTLEMENT AND PLACE NAMES

Despite having two small Roman forts, Exmoor was never really Romanised. Iron Age settlements continued in use throughout the Roman period and there appears to have been continuity of use of the same land units, if not the same settlement sites, for much longer. Medieval and earlier settlements are associated with Iron Age earthworks at Road near Exford; Spangate, on the southern side of Dunkery Hill, and Sweetworthy, on its northern side, which also shows evidence of farming and settlement from Iron Age until the nineteenth century.

Most Exmoor place names are Saxon or medieval in origin, but the Celtic language survived locally well into Saxon times and beyond. Combe, similar to the Welsh *cwm*, means a valley; Minehead may come from *mynedd*, meaning a large hill; the Hangman Hills may come from *an maen*, meaning a stony hill or cairn.

Below: Iron Age fortifications top Wind Hill (courtesy National Trust)

LOCAL NAMES

There are many locally distinctive names for landscape features: 'ball' for a rounded hillside spur such as Wimbleball, which means the ball where windle grass grows; 'cleave' for a steep valley side such as Myrtleberry Cleave, which is the cleave where whortleberry grows; 'gut' such as Great Hangman Gut, means a gully; 'girt' such as Pudleep Girt, means a steep little valley; 'bottom' as in Charles, Galloping and Velvet Bottoms, means the bottom of a valley, and 'brake' as in Cornham Brake, is a bracken-covered hillside.

The distribution of settlements of different sizes tends to be linked with the pattern of farming. Apart from market towns, boroughs and other places not directly dependent on farming, Exmoor villages largely grew up in arable farming areas. This was partly because of the practices of sharing out the better land between farms and pooling labour, plough animals and equipment in arable areas. Hamlets tended to develop in mixed farming areas and are often surrounded by old enclosures. Many have shrunk in recent years, as mixed farming has turned purely pastoral and less labour intensive. Isolated farmsteads usually represent former colonisation of waste land and moorland. The nineteenth-century enclosure of common land resulted in the establishment of new farmsteads in the centre of compact groups of large square fields. Hamlets are, however, the norm on Exmoor and many of the older isolated farms are likely to have been the centres of hamlets at the height of rural population in the mid-ninteenth century.

Most Exmoor villages originated in Saxon times. This was a period of colonisation, clearance of woodland and arable farming in relatively small open fields, long since enclosed as pasture. Place names ending in 'ton' are evidence of villages of that period. Such villages are few and far between, partly because of the lack of land suited to arable farming and partly because of continuing Celtic occupation. A 'barton' was a large family farm, isolated and more typical of the Saxon occupation of Exmoor.

As land was divided between heirs, smaller farms developed from bartons to form hamlets or outlying farms. The thirteenth century appears to have been a period of rapid population expansion on Exmoor, as elsewhere in the country, and much waste land was taken into cultivation. The 'cott' and 'worthy' place names so common on Exmoor relate to farms and hamlets of this period. The Black Death in the fourteenth century was a setback, but nothing like in most parts of England and, unusually, the breaking of new ground seems to have continued. Moorland settlements at Badgworthy, Lank Combe and Bagley may have been deserted indirectly through the Black Death, in that as such poor land became exhausted, death released land in more fertile areas. Another reason may be the emphasis on sheep farming. Lower population meant reduced prices for grain and less labour for arable farming. Lords of manors, lacking in manpower and markets for crops, let much of their land to tenants for enclosure and improvement. Improved communications allowed for the import of grain and export of wool, and a rationalisation of farming to concentrate on what best suited the area.

Above: Cow Castle: an Iron Age hill fort in the Barle valley
Opposite: Challacombe Barton and mill: a typical Exmoor settlement

COMMUNICATIONS

Many of today's roads follow prehistoric routes and part of the Harepath is reputed to be among the country's best preserved examples of an ancient track. Early routes were along ridges and settlement was typically close to these routes but below the exposed tops, on the spring lines above the valley sides. The numerous 'twitchen' names indicate places where side routes split from the main route. Valleys were avoided as they were thickly wooded, steep-sided and prone to

flooding. However, grist and woollen mills later developed in the valley bottoms and so did tracks linking them with farms. Tracks also developed linking isolated farms and hamlets with churches and villages. The scattered nature of the settlement is reflected in the great network of tiny country lanes today.

Old routes were often greatly improved for the medieval wool trade and many stone bridges originated as a result. Packhorse bridges are typically narrow as wheeled traffic was not possible on most upland parts of Exmoor until the nineteenth century. As engineering methods improved, later roads, particularly the nineteenth century turnpikes, followed the valleys. Water powered all kinds of machinery and irrigated fertile meadows and settlement began to grow in the valleys, often to the detriment of the original settlement around the church. At Parracombe, Upton and Brendon, new churches were built in more convenient locations and in some new settlements nonconformist churches grew to rival the parish churches. The original settlement at Parracombe remains with the old church, as Churchtown and the village consists of four hamlets joined along roads.

CHURCHES

The size and style of Exmoor churches reflects the wealth of the parishes. Its churches tend to be small in the farming areas on the moor and larger in the surrounding manufacturing and market areas exploiting such farming. Culbone, Trentishoe, Withycombe and Withiel Florey are all good examples of simple moorland churches in the local style.

The dedications of several Exmoor churches to Celtic saints such as Petrock , Beuno, Brendan, Dubricius and Salwyn suggest origins before Domesday. However, few of the present churches have parts dating from earlier than the thirteenth century. Crosses were often the original sites from which the gospel was preached, and churches were sometimes later built on the northern sides of such crosses. Exmoor is lucky in that several survived their widespread removal or desecration in the Reformation. Luxborough may have the oldest: its shaft is possibly Saxon. There are also fragments of a Saxon cross in Porlock church and a Saxon window at Culbone. St George's at Dunster was probably the first Norman church on Exmoor. There are good Norman doorways there and at Hawkridge, which also has a Norman font, as does West Anstey church. Most older Exmoor churches were made entirely of local stone rubble. Later some better stone was imported for monuments, decoration and restoration. The best

Above: Packhorse bridge at Allerford
Opposite: The Harepath at Great Vintcombe: a well-preserved, prehistoric trackway
Below: Britain's smallest parish church at Culbone
Pages 54-5: Dunster Castle from the Deer Park

HUNTING PARSONS

The doggerel verse 'Culbone, Oare and Stoke Pero, parishes three no parson'l go to', reflects the fact that the living of such sparsely populated moorland parishes was too poor to support a parson without independent means. No wonder the area is famed for its 'hunting parsons' such as Jack Russell, who had enough money and few demands from their professional duties to allow them to enjoy their sport.

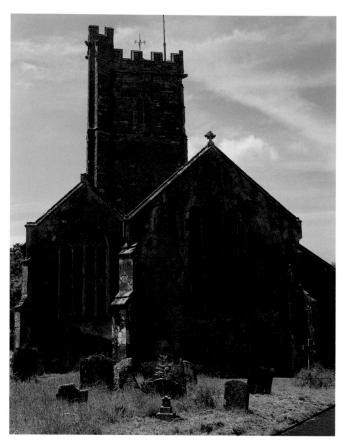

Above: Churchyard cross at Exford
Above right: Perpendicular windows at Luccombe

monuments are at Porlock and Nettlecombe, where there is also a rare and beautiful fifteenth-century font. Medieval floor tiles can be seen at Luccombe and Timberscombe, where there is also a medieval door.

To find local character, you must look at churches which escaped Victorian restoration. These are largely Perpendicular in their style. Many were rebuilt in the late fifteenth and early sixteenth centuries during the fashion for Gothic architecture, when the Church was at the height of its wealth and power. At this time, towers and porches were added to simple moorland churches which previously had only a nave, where the congregation stood, and a chancel for the altar, priest and choir. The larger churches on the Exmoor fringes usually had additional accommodation for the congregation in aisles running either side of the nave at the same length and height as the nave. These are known as 'hall churches,' and to these were also added side chapels. The standard plan of chancel, nave (with or without aisles), west tower and south porch is characteristic of Devon and West Somerset. Towers are square, solid and simple, more typical of Devon than the famous Decorated and pinnacled towers of Somerset. Porches to the larger churches sometimes had a room above for a priest or school, such as those at Porlock and Selworthy.

Selworthy church has beautiful Perpendicular architecture, among the finest in the West Country, and Luccombe church has particularly ornate Perpendicular windows. On the Exmoor fringes are exceptionally fine, ornately carved wooden rood screens dating from this period, particularly at Dunster, Carhampton, Combe Martin and Minehead, which retains its rood loft. Rood screens, which divided the chancel from the nave, were often removed during the Reformation or later restoration, but survived here better than elsewhere. The rood loft, which carried a gallery over the screen with the rood, a depiction of Calvary, was a particular target for Puritan reformists and rarely survives in Britain.

In some churches seating was marked for the occupants of hamlets and farms within the parish. Chapels of ease are common in hamlets within large parishes where it was argued that winter journeys to church were difficult. Anglican chapels of ease can be seen at Lynch and Tivington (thatched) in Selworthy parish and at Leighland, which was once a parish church serving a mining population which has now disappeared. If they did not have chapels of ease large parishes, particularly in Devon, often had church houses. These were buildings in or adjoining the churchyards which provided refreshment and a place to rest for churchgoers travelling from outlying parts of the parish. They often sold ale too for church funds and became village pubs. Those at Parracombe and Martinhoe have been converted for accommodation.

INDUSTRIAL BUILDINGS

For a quiet, rural area, Exmoor has had a surprisingly rich industrial past. Who would believe, for instance, that it once had the world's largest copper mine or was an important centre of the woollen industry, more usually associated with the north of England? Dunster's famous Yarn Market was built for sale of the local tweed cloth, and many old corn mills started life as tucking or fulling mills, used for the washing of wools and finishing of cloth.

The harbour at Porlock Weir was improved for the export of Exmoor minerals. It has lock gates to hold water in the harbour at low tide and allow for a safer and more leisurely transfer of cargoes. The mineral trade never really materialised, but charcoal from local woods was exported for the smelting industries of south Wales and coal and limestone were brought back in return. The Weir gets its name not from the harbour but from the fish traps or 'weirs' on the beach. For centuries

TAKING A PEW

Pews did not really come in until the sixteenth century and most were thrown out by Victorians, but good early furniture survives at Brushford, Culbone, Molland, Parracombe and West Anstey. The growing population in the eighteenth and nineteenth centuries often led to the addition of galleries at the west end of the nave. A good early example of this is at Countisbury, and there are musicians' galleries at Trentishoe and St Petrock's, Parracombe.

Left: Dunster Mill beside the River Avill

these were a common form of fishing on the Bristol Channel coast, making use of the great tidal range. The weirs take the form of two low walls of beach pebbles arranged in a V shape pointing in the direction of the ebbing tide. Originally there were wattle fences on top of the walls and the apex of the V had a gap across which a net was strung. As the tide receded, the fish in the area covered by the weir were forced into the net. Several on the Exmoor coast have medieval or earlier origins and one, for catching salmon at the mouth of the Lyn, still operates.

Great use was made on Exmoor of water power, particularly for mills, sawmills, forges and farm machinery. Lynton and Lynmouth were the first settlement in Britain to have hydro-electric power, which continued until the 1952 flood destroyed the power station. It included one of the first pumped storage schemes. A water-powered railway is still in use there. Two cars on parallel tracks are attached via a pulley and counterbalanced by water tanks so that the descending car pulls the other one up. It was the world's steepest railway when it was built in 1890 and was used as much then for carrying goods for Lynton from the harbour at Lynmouth as it is for carrying tourists now.

LIME KILNS

Writing his *Survey of Devon* in the early seventeenth century, Tristram Risdon said of lime kilns: 'of late, a new invention hath sprung up'. In fact, they were by no means a new invention, having been used for thousands of years, but their local use for agriculture was new and the name stuck. Names such as 'New Invention', 'Invention' or simply 'Vention' imply lime kilns, although until the middle of the eighteenth century such structures were only temporary and have long since disappeared.

Below: Eighteenth-century lime kiln and lime burner's cottage at Woody Bay

Those now found on Exmoor were in use at sometime between the 1780s and 1920s. The lime came into great demand when the Napoleonic Wars forced up grain prices and brought much new land into cultivation. It continued to be required locally because of the spate of enclosure and moorland reclamation in the mid-nineteenth century.

Exmoor lime kilns are mostly of a type known as continuous draw kilns. They consist of a large cone-shaped 'pot' which contained layers of limestone and 'culm' (anthracite dust) to fire it. Air was let in at draw holes in the base of the structure, through which burnt lime and ash were raked out. The kilns are mostly built with rounded draw holes suited to the rough local stone. As material was extracted, more lime and fuel were added and the whole was kept burning continually. This produced a poor quality lime, as it was mixed with ash, but suited agricultural purposes. Some kilns produced better quality lime for cement, plaster and lime wash. Local limestone was used at places like Combe Martin, Newlands and Treborough, but kilns on the coast used Welsh lime and culm, brought in by small boats. Some are in spectacular locations, such as at Heddon's Mouth, Rodney and Embelle, where access was treacherous. Sailing ketches would tie to mooring posts at high tide and dump their cargoes overboard, to be recovered at low tide.

THE ACLANDS

The Aclands were Exmoor's great landowning dynasty. From their fifteenth-century origins at Acland Barton near Landkey, male heirs in each generation married wealthy heiresses and their property steadily amassed. When the second Sir Thomas – known as 'His Honour' – came into his inheritance in the late eighteenth century, he owned much of central Exmoor. His estate included the Pixton, Highercombe and Holnicote estates and properties southwards towards Exeter, and he boasted that he could ride the 30 miles from Killerton to Holnicote on his own land.

The first Sir Thomas took an interest in hunting and set up the first pack of stag hounds to be kennelled on the moor. Holnicote became a hunting lodge. The first three Sir Thomases were wardens of the Royal Forest and did much to improve the area. The third Sir Thomas received an allotment of 3,200 acres (1,295ha) on its sale and he was the saviour of the Exmoor pony when he took 400 ponies from the Forest to set up the core herd on Winsford Hill. Today this is known as the Anchor herd from his anchor-shaped brand. Known as 'The Great Sir Thomas' he developed the *cottage ornée* architecture of the Holnicote estate, rebuilt the thatched cottages on the green at Selworthy for estate pensioners and, through his nurseryman and landscape consultant, John Veitch, planted well over a million exotic and native trees. His grandson, one of the first Forestry Commissioners, created some of the earliest commercial conifer plantations.

The nineteenth-century Aclands were benevolent landlords with a concern for politics and public works. They tended to be ahead of their time and often forsook their careers for the sake of principle.

THE KNIGHTS

In contrast to landed gentry like the Aclands, the Knights were the *nouveau riche* of their day. John Knight had inherited money from the Midlands iron industry and aspired to become a country squire. When the King's Allotment, the largest part of the Royal Forest of Exmoor, came up for sale in 1818, he seized the chance to acquire an estate of over 10,000 acres (4,000ha). Within two years he had

SAVIOUR OF EXMOOR

The end of a long tradition of family landownership came with Sir Richard Acland. A socialist politician and founder of the Common Wealth party, he espoused principles of shared ownership and gave his Killerton and Holnicote estates to the nation via the National Trust in 1944. Without their protection of the 10,000 acre (4,000ha) Holnicote estate, containing much of Exmoor's most characteristic scenery, architecture and wildlife, Exmoor may not have become a National Park.

Opposite: Characteristic buildings:
Cottage at Selworthy (Courtesy
National Trust)
Below: Pinkworthy Pond: one of John
Knight's 'white elephants'

bought out neighbouring land, increasing the property by half as much again. Following the Enclosure Act of 1815, he was legally bound to enclose the former Forest and make roads. By 1824 he had encircled his property with walls and banks over 30 miles diameter and metalled miles of roads radiating from Simonsbath.

Inspired by the pioneers of the Agrarian revolution, such as the Dukes of Bedford and Coke of Norfolk, he set about improving the land. Copying neighbouring estates, he started on the better soils the local way – cutting and burning the turf, turning over the soil and leaving it to weather, draining where necessary, and liming. He then made the mistake of trying to apply the Norfolk four-course rotation of crops for growing corn and lost out to the fickle Exmoor weather. He also tried introducing new breeds of stock such as Hereford cattle, Merino sheep, Arab horses and Westphalian pigs, with the same effect. Even the Irish labourers did not suit and his dam at Pinkworthy and mansion at Simonsbath became white elephants.

John's son, Frederic, was more of a pioneer, adapting new methods to local conditions. Working with experienced local agents, he used traditional earth banks to enclose large new fields, local stone to build new model farms and steam ploughs to break the soil before planting root crops or rape to improve for grass in the local manner. He made some mistakes, such as attempts at mining and creating a deer park but, through his trick of letting land to tenants on condition that they improved it, he did not suffer the financial losses of his father. He created farms, introduced hardy northern breeds of sheep and cattle and kept the breeding stock through the winter, setting the basic pattern of stock rearing on Exmoor which still exists today.

4 Land use, culture and customs

Top: *Judging Exmoor Horn sheep at Dunster Show*
Centre: *Sheep sales at Cutcombe Market*
Above: *Devon cattle at Dunster Show*

It is difficult to separate the works of man and nature in the Exmoor landscape. The whole appearance of the countryside depends on skills which are part of the local culture. The moorland itself is a product of centuries-old farming practices. Even different farm animals have their own effect on the vegetation, and breeds like the Exmoor Horn and Devon Closewool sheep, Red Devon cattle and Exmoor ponies all contribute to local distinctiveness. The numbers employed in agriculture are in decline and farming has long been replaced by service industries as the main source of employment on Exmoor. As machines replace labour, it is not easy to keep the skills necessary to maintain the character of Exmoor.

The Exmoor National Park Authority pioneered management agreement schemes which compensate landowners and farmers for conservation measures and for any loss of income they may suffer from farming the land less intensively. Such schemes have largely been superseded by more widespread government schemes like the Environmentally Sensitive Area and Countryside Stewardship schemes, administered by the Ministry of Agriculture. The National Park Authority runs its own Farm Conservation Scheme and provides grants for conservation measures not covered by the other schemes. Hill farming is becoming increasingly dependent on these schemes as headage payments for stock give way to acreage payments and Exmoor's relatively small farms lose out.

Many moorland dairy farms lost out in terms of economy of scale, and only a handful remain on the fringes of Exmoor. Most of its farmland is pasture for sheep and beef cattle. Exmoor cattle are grass fed and free of BSE, but the disease has depressed beef farming generally. There are attempts to revive the trade by labelling local beef as the quality product it is. At the time of writing the value of wool is hardly greater than the cost of shearing and demand for lamb is also low. Exmoor farmers have held their own by buying the markets at Barnstaple, Blackmoor Gate and Cutcombe and keeping the businesses viable. Dealers now come from all over the country to buy fat lambs and store cattle. The Vale of Porlock still produces excellent malting barley and other corn crops, and several Exmoor farmers are turning over to mixed organic farming. Other diversification has included game crops, fish farming, deer farming, even ostriches and a vineyard.

Many local businesses are still dependent on farming and forestry, such as contractors and engineers, sawmilling, fencing, nurseries and feed merchants, and there are new firms producing stock handling equipment, veterinary supplies and electronic cattle tagging. Many businesses also depend on horse riding and would be severely hit if hunting was banned. However, new technology is enabling small local businesses to compete more effectively and there is some light industry, including light engineering, paper making, scientific instrument making, tea and coffee blending and wood working.

Tourism is the main industry on Exmoor, and the tourist market is seen as one way of keeping craft traditions alive. Exmoor offers many good examples of the positive approach towards tourism in attempting to make it sustainable – benefiting both environment and community. There is encouragement for tourists to purchase local products and sample food produced on Exmoor. Those marketing

Exmoor for tourism are being encouraged to do so for its natural attractions and not to promote development which is out of character or harms the environment. While tourists come for Exmoor's special qualities, they will help to sustain the industries which keep it special.

Above: Vineyard at Wootton Courtenay

THE LIVING CULTURE

Customs bind the local community and help to make it culturally distinct. Many Exmoor customs revolved around the farming year but are dying out due to changes in farming methods. There was Plough Monday in January, when plough horses were decorated to signal the return to work after festivities. Then there were Lady Day and Michaelmas – farm rent days when estate owners treated their tenants to traditional meals. Shearing ended with feasting and dancing and after harvest, the 'crying the neck' custom, where the holder of a corn dolly ran the gauntlet from cornfield to church. Still practised is the wassailing of apple trees on Old Twelfth Night to ensure a good crop of cider apples and burning an 'ashen faggot' on Christmas Eve to ensure prosperity the following season.

Food is also something which is changing. In the past it much depended upon ingredients and the means of cooking locally available. The production of clotted cream, for instance, was suited to the once-common, slow-burning peat fires and was a method of preserving the small quantities of cream produced until there was enough to sell at market. Laver is an edible seaweed found only in commercial

ARTISTS OF EXMOOR

Many artists and craftsmen who can work from home have chosen Exmoor as a pleasant place to live. There are potters, weavers, furniture makers, artists and designers, writers, needlecraft workers, wrought iron and glass makers. European grants have helped to raise the profile of local craft products.

Above: Point -to-point race at
Holnicote
Opposite: Meet of the Exmoor
Foxhounds at Simonsbath

quantities in the Bristol Channel where the great tidal range extends its habitat in the middle part of the shore. It is sold pickled as a condiment for fried meals and hog's pudding, a poor man's sausage packed with grain, and was the main ingredient of a sauce to accompany the once-famed moorland mutton.

Exmoor people are immersed in equestrian culture and there is every sort of hunting, eventing, point to points, gymkhanas and shows. Notable are the Exmoor Spring Horse Show, Exmoor Pony Society Stallion Parade and the Golden Horseshoe national endurance event, all held in May, and the Exmoor Carriage Driving Festival in July. Bampton Fair originated as a horse sale and the Brendon Pony Fair is still very much linked with horses. At most shows there are competitive riding events and demonstrations of country pursuits and many events are linked with hunts. Several packs of hounds hunt fox, stag, hare, mink and buck and hunting of some kind takes place daily through much of the year except during May, June and July and on Sundays. The stag hunts in particular involve many

FETES WORSE THAN DEATH

Many village fetes and shows are survivors of the former revels which marked the days of the saints to which their churches were dedicated. In their heyday, they were drunken, rowdy affairs. Male muscle was tested in wrestling bouts and fisticuffs and there were even contests between adversaries armed with cudgels. Those which survived Victorian disapproval, such as at Hawkridge and Parracombe, are now much tamer affairs, as is the Earl of Rone ceremony at Combe Martin and the Hobby Horse at Minehead, where the processions still include calls at local pubs

Left: The Earl of Rone ceremony at Combe Martin

hundreds of riders and motorised followers and there can be much congestion as a result. There is a West Somerset Polo Club and there are regular matches at the Carnarvon Arms at Brushford. Details of events can be found in local newspapers.

ENCLOSURES

On Exmoor there is little stone for walling and earth enclosures prevail. They vary greatly in age and design. The nine-course bank was supposedly laid by a team of nine men, each adding a layer of earth and a course of facing stones. The earth was dug from ditching either side of the bank, thus providing drainage and effectively increasing the height of the bank. 'Ditching' is also the term for laying the facing stones on edge. In the west, the stones were sometimes laid in Cornish herringbone fashion and 'dykes' were dug into hillsides like terraces, with only one side to be faced with stone. They are generally very old, having been superseded by beech hedgebanks.

Beech grows at greater altitude on Exmoor than elsewhere and was advocated by the Acland family for sheltering moorland stock, as the dead leaves remain on the trees throughout winter. Most of the hedgebanks accompanied Parliamentary enclosure of common land. This came late to Exmoor as only in the nineteenth century, with new methods including rotations of root crops, did Exmoor's moorland seem improvable, then only for pasture. Wheeled traffic was not common on upland Exmoor until such Enclosure Acts brought better roads. They were a regulation 40ft (12.2m) wide between hedgebanks, including a 12ft (3.7m) road surface and wide verges to allow for the passing of flocks of sheep. Frequently there are long narrow enclosures alongside such roads to allow for the resting of animals being driven long distances.

The large, rectangular Parliamentary enclosures contrast with the small, irregular earlier fields which resulted from the piecemeal enclosure of waste land. Old enclosures, often dating from Saxon or medieval times, are found around Exmoor hamlets and villages and enclosures generally become younger away from such settlements. Remains of even older enclosures are associated with prehistoric settlement and some date back 3,000 years or more. Barbed wire came into wide use on Exmoor in the 1890s, at the start of a long depression in agriculture, and proved cheaper than maintaining the hedgebanks.

STEEPING THE HEDGES

Exmoor hedges need to be maintained by 'steeping' or laying to keep them stockproof and by throwing earth onto the bank, which serves to root the laid branches. This process is skilled, time consuming and expensive. Conservation grants have helped to make up the difference in cost and new laws will, hopefully, help to protect the most important hedgebanks for their wildlife or historical value.

Top: 'Stone walling': John Richards faces an earth hedgebank at Culbone
Above: Roadside enclosure in the Brendon Hills

BUILDINGS

Many characteristic Exmoor cottages and farmhouses are medieval in origin but show later changes. Some developed from the 'cross passage' pattern – divided by a straight passage running from front to back door. Here the pattern was of three rooms, with two family rooms side by side and divided from the other by the cross passage. Buildings often ran downhill but rarely in the 'longhouse' style, with cattle in the lower part. Old buildings are of local materials, as transport of heavy goods was virtually impossible except along the coast. Most are made of uncoursed stone rubble, as Exmoor stone is unevenly textured and cannot be cut neatly. The crooked and stunted sessile oaks of Exmoor produced curved timbers for boats but were of little of use for buildings. Small quantities of ashlar (dressed stone) were imported for public buildings and wealthy houses, as quoins for windows, doorways and chimneys. Many Exmoor buildings had rounded chimneys and supports to avoid this expense. In Victorian and Edwardian times, brick tended to replace ashlar. In the west, particularly around Combe Martin, much use was made of cream coloured bricks from the Marland clay pits of North Devon.

The local red sandstone is porous and walls are treated with lime plaster and wash, which prevents some ingress of water while allowing the walls to 'breathe'. Those facing the prevailing south-westerlies are often hung with slates. Cob walls prevail where there is a lack of stone and plentiful supply of clay. Cob is mostly clay but may be worked with dung, straw or horse hair or mixed with lime for plastering walls and ceilings and as mortar for stonework. Lime ash, the waste from lime burning, was mixed with water to make a form of concrete for flooring. Cob buildings tend to have thick walls with no sharp corners, small windows cut straight out of the cob and overhanging roofs and tarred plinths to protect against rain and frost.

Pantiles are ridged tiles which overlap sideways as well as vertically and run in vertical rows, rather than being staggered like slates. They overlap less than other tiles and produce a light roof suited to replacing thatch with its weak supports. Bridgwater was a centre of their manufacture and they are more common to the east of Exmoor. Slates were produced locally at Treborough and other small quarries. Their use is traditional on the exposed western parts of the moor where the long thatching corn could not be grown.

FARM BUILDINGS

Unlike its other buildings, in Exmoor's farm buildings a vernacular, or distinctive local style, survived until the late nineteenth century. Unfortunately, most cannot be adapted for modern farming and some are falling to ruin or have been converted to other accommodation. Many were made of materials such as wood, cob and thatch – which soon decay without maintenance. Even with stone buildings, few built before the middle of the seventeenth century survive, exceptions being the medieval tithe barns and dovecotes of Dunster and Selworthy.

EXMOOR THATCH

Thatch is a relatively light material which suits weak, stony cob walls. However, the Exmoor tradition is to add new layers rather than replace thatch, and roofs become thick and heavy with age, often requiring strengthening. Thatch allows valleys and dormers to be incorporated into the roofs, which do not easily adapt to other materials. Where tiles replace thatch there is often an unsightly mass of downpipes and gutters. Some thatching wheat is grown on Exmoor but the old, long straw wheat varieties do not suit modern fertilisers or machinery. A return to organic farming may help.

Left: Thatched farm buildings at Tivington Knowle
Above: Typical cottages at Luccombe
Pages 68-9: Beech hedgebank at Chetsford Bridge (courtesy National Trust)

Right: Thatched linhay at Bossington
Below: 'Shelley's cottage' at
Lynmouth

The pastoral farming of the uplands required few buildings compared with the mixed farming of the Vale of Porlock and northern edge of the Brendon Hills, where the greatest variety survives. However, corn – particularly oats – was grown for winter food for humans and animals and straw for bedding and thatching. Every farm had a barn for threshing corn and storing straw. Such barns are usually the most ancient and distinctive buildings still found. Separate granaries are rare, as the precious grain was kept in the farmhouse except where plentiful, such as in the Vale of Porlock, where there were also corn drying and barley malting kilns. Some farms had rounded sheds for 'horse machines,' where horses walked to drive machinery for threshing or cider pressing in adjacent barns.

Every farmer rode a horse, although few were used for heavy farm work until the nineteenth century, and so most farms had a small stable and shippon for the working oxen. Young cattle were folded in the farm yard for the winter and often farm buildings were formed into quadrangles to shelter the yard. Linhays, with enclosed hay lofts above, sheltered the cattle in the fields. Elsewhere hay barns tend to be open and separate, but linhays evolved to suit the wet and windy climate. They were often built into a south-facing hillside and the stone which was excavated was used for the building. The upper storey was often supported in front by rounded pillars, which suited the rough, uncut stone.

THE ARTS

Writers of all kinds have been attracted by the Exmoor landscape and its wildlife. The area became a Mecca for students following in the footsteps of the Romantic poets and seeking their own inspiration. Shelley came to Lynmouth in 1812 and stayed for an extended honeymoon with his teenage bride. Much has been written about the wild red deer, in particular by historian John Fortescue and wildlife authors Richard Jeffries and Henry Williamson. Part of Williamson's *Tarka the Otter* was set on Exmoor, as was his *Gale of the World*, which was about the Lynmouth flood disaster of 1952. The footsteps of Tarka over Exmoor are now followed by a long distance walking trail set up to bring sustainable tourism to the area. Novels of R.F. Delderfield and R.D. Blackmore were inspired by their schooldays on Exmoor and the Rev W.H. Thornton's *Reminiscences of an old West*

Country Clergyman is a classic of its kind, providing much insight into the life of Exmoor in the mid-ninteeenth century.

Exmoor is reputed to have been the inspiration for Mrs Alexander's hymn, 'All Things Bright and Beautiful', and it was home to tinker poet Dicky Slader, who wrote the words to many hymns. Cecil Sharp collected many folk songs from the Exmoor area, where several towns have music and folk festivals. Painter Sir Alfred Munnings spent his war years on Exmoor and sporting artists Lionel Jeffries and Cecil Aldin came purely for the pleasure the area gave them.

Above: Grabbist Hill and the Avill valley: alleged inspiration for 'All Things Bright and Beautiful'

ROMANTIC ARTS

Exmoor was largely unknown to the outside world until the end of the eighteenth century, when several events conspired to change that situation. The first was the Romantic Movement in the arts with its aesthetic appreciation of the landscape, which inspired architecture on the Holnicote and Glenthorne estates. The second were the Napoleonic wars, which forced the wealthy who normally took cultural tours of Europe to look at their own country. Several well known figures in the arts, including painters Gainsborough and Turner, visited Exmoor and, through their enthusiasm for its landscape, helped to put it on the map.

A group of poet friends - Coleridge, Wordsworth and Southey - made several visits. Coleridge lived at Nether Stowey on the Quantocks from 1796 to 1798 and often walked along the coast to Exmoor. While staying at a farm near Culbone, the

poem *Kubla Khan* came to him as a vision after he had taken opium for what he described as 'dysentery'. When he came out of his stupor he started to write down the poem from memory, only to be disturbed by a 'person from Porlock', after whose visit he could recall little more. His descriptions of 'forests ancient as the hills' and 'a sunless sea' were possibly inspired by Culbone, as were parts of *Osorio*, such as 'The hanging woods, most lovely in decay, The many clouds, the Sea, the Rock, the Sands'. Wordsworth came to live near him in 1797 and they spent several days exploring Exmoor and inspiring one another to write, during which time they worked on *The Rime of the Ancient Mariner*.

The wives of Southey and Coleridge were sisters and Southey came to Exmoor on a family visit. He never forgot the area and returned in later life. He wrote a sonnet *To Porlock* while wet weather confined him at the Ship Inn there. He was chiefly remembered for his diaries and his glowing descriptions of Lynmouth and the Valley of Rocks were much used to attract tourists. His likening of the area to Switzerland sparked a fashion in Swiss architecture. Essayist Charles Lamb and critic William Hazlitt also visited Coleridge. Hazlitt walked with him to the Valley of Rocks, describing it as 'bedded among precipices overhanging the sea, with rocky caverns beneath, into which the waves dash, and where the seagull forever wheels its screaming flight'.

FOLKLORE

Exmoor's best known folk stories surround the Doones, a legendary band of outlaws. Stories collected early in the nineteenth century were later used by R.D. Blackmore in his novel *Lorna Doone*. Many have attempted to trace the ancestry of Lorna and the Doones and place them in real life seventeenth-century Exmoor. The same goes for Tom Faggus, another character in the novel. Tom was a North Molton blacksmith until he lost his business in a lawsuit with the local squire. He became a local Robin Hood figure as a highwayman, robbing the rich to help the poor and never harming anyone. He was always accompanied by his strawberry mare, Winnie, who helped him evade capture on many occasions when he whistled for her assistance. Once she is said to have carried him over the parapet of Barnstaple Bridge into the Taw. She had to be shot before he could be caught.

There are also many legends surrounding local saints and religious customs. One surrounds Jesus, who is said to have visited as a boy on a trading excursion with Joseph of Arimathea. Looking for water, He found the spot where Joseph plunged his staff into the ground to create Sisters' Fountain spring at Glenthorne. Joseph returned on the way to Glastonbury with the Holy Grail.

The most recent legend surrounds the 'beast of Exmoor.' This started in 1983 with a spate of sheep killings around the southern edge of the moor. The carcasses had been stripped from the neck down, suggesting that the culprit was a big cat, such as a puma or panther. A national newspaper offered a reward for capture or a photograph of the 'beast' and the hunt was on. So frequent were the killings that Royal Marines with rifles and night sights were engaged at one point. They were convinced that a large dog was the culprit, but none was found. Killings continued all over Exmoor and North Devon, some so far apart but close in time that one animal could not have been responsible. Since then there have been many reports of big cats – brown, black and spotted. Many sensible people have had good sightings and are convinced there is something out there. Today there is even a Beast Society.

THE DEVIL'S WORK

The Devil was used to account for many otherwise unexplainable objects. The Valley of Rocks has many such stories, and its main ridge is known as Rugged Jack, after the leader of a group of drunkards making merry and breaking the Sabbath. The Devil, wishing to join in, was annoyed at not being recognised and turned them all to stone. He is also supposed to have created the Punchbowl on Winsford Hill, the Whitstones on Porlock Hill and Tarr Steps clapper bridge. He stopped people crossing the bridge while he sunbathed on it and only allowed its public use after he lost a 'slanging match' with a parson.

Above: Rugged Jack in the Valley of Rocks: reputed to be the work of the Devil
Opposite: Overgrown beech hedgebanks on Twitchen Ridge
Pages 74-5: May Day hobby horse ceremony at Dunster

5 Recreation

Above: Walkers on Ashton Cleave
Opposite: Hot air balloons on North Common

National Parks are often regarded as the 'lungs' of the nation, and were intended as places to which town dwellers could resort for fresh air and healthy outdoor exercise and to recover from the stresses of daily life. All too often, however, the modern tourist comes by car, and the main activity seems to be driving around sightseeing, which often includes themed tourist attractions rather than the appreciation of the countryside. Amazingly, half of the visitors to Exmoor are merely passing through.

There is beauty and fascination all around you in the National Parks, and it is surely better to stop and stare than dash about. As long ago as 1810, William Wordsworth had advocated that the Lake District should be 'a sort of national property, in which every man has a right and interest who has an eye to perceive and a heart to enjoy'. If you do go sightseeing, public transport is better for the environment, for seeing the countryside, and for meeting people. It is also an aid to exploring Exmoor on foot, because it does not confine walkers to the busy circular routes from car parks. The Exmoor National Park Authority provides timetables containing suggestions for walks, leaflets which help you plan your days out by bus and guided walks based on bus routes. These are available from Visitor Centres.

After sightseeing by car, the main activity is sightseeing on foot. Few who stop on Exmoor do not walk a mile or more. Exmoor is not mountainous and it appears gentle and beautiful enough to tempt the laziest persons from their cars. Many look for 'a walk' as if locations offer just one walk. However, with over 600 miles (1,000km) of rights of way, Exmoor has a network of routes which can be tailored to anyone's walking needs. There are plenty of guides and leaflets, but Exmoor is a place to explore and discover, so it is often more rewarding to buy a map and plan your own route.

ACCESS

Exmoor's rights of way are generally well maintained and signposted but, in order to maintain the feeling of wilderness, signs and waymarks are limited on open moorland. The National Park Authority introduced the system of waymarking to Britain in the early 1960s. Waymarks are coloured squares or arrows helping walkers and others to follow routes in places where navigation is difficult. They also distinguish the way in which routes may be used: yellow markers denote routes for walkers only; blue routes can also be used by cyclists and horse riders, and red routes by motor vehicles. White markers are used on 'permissive' (permitted) routes where access has been negotiated with landowners and is not a legal right. Exmoor also has three long distance trails with their own waymarks: the Tarka Trail with an otter's paw mark; the Two Moors Way with a 'MW' mark,

NATIONAL, NOT NATIONALISED

Despite their name, British National Parks are not public property and 75 per cent of Exmoor is privately owned. However, they do provide a greater freedom of access than comparable parts of England and Wales. The Exmoor National Park Authority is a major landowner and provides open access to much of its property, which amounts to 7 per cent of the Park, as does the National Trust, which owns over 10 per cent.

Right: South West Coast Path at Countisbury Hill
Below: Public transport at Luccombe
Below right: Tarka Trail waymark at Broad Mead
Pages 80-1: The South West Coast Path winds its way along cliff tops at Trentishoe Down (courtesy National Trust)

and the South West Coast Path with the acorn mark of all National Trails.

It is best to keep to the rights of way marked on Ordnance Survey maps unless you are sure that you have permission to do otherwise. Exmoor differs from its neighbour, Dartmoor, in that there is not necessarily a right of open access to common land, except to a handful of commons in former urban districts, including the Valley of Rocks, Ilkerton, Furzehill and Alcombe Commons. The Government has announced its intention to allow public access to all open country in England and Wales. This may include most of Exmoor's moorland and heath and possibly also much woodland, seashore and open water. At present, the Ordnance Survey Outdoor Leisure Map of Exmoor shows some open access areas and 'permissive' routes, and National Park Visitor Centres can help with route planning.

THE SOUTH WEST COAST PATH

The South West Coast Path is the longest of the National Trails of England and Wales. These trails are designated by the Countryside Agency, which grant aids the local authorities through whose areas they run. The trail starts at Minehead and runs along the whole of the 34 miles (54km) of the Exmoor coastline and on around the West Country to Poole in Dorset, a total length of 613 miles (980km). Few walk the whole trail but you would miss out on some of Exmoor's most spectacular scenery if you did not take in at least part of it.

Although the trail looks fairly smooth on the map, the coastline is high and punctuated by valleys. In walking the whole trail, you would have to climb over 91,000ft (28,000m), so don't bite off more than you can chew! The easiest part is probably the Valley of Rocks. You can start at Lynton and walk one way along the trail at North Walk and the other way along the road, all quite level and tarmaced and only two miles in all. A spectacular variation is to walk out over Hollerday Hill, from behind Lynton's Town Hall. Another level part of the trail is around Porlock Bay between Bossington and Porlock Weir. At present, the breach in the shingle ridge has caused a diversion inland through Porlock, but this makes a more varied walk. It is best to start at Allerford or Porlock Weir and make the return journey by bus. Buses run along part of the coast throughout the year and the whole length between June and September, making circular walks unnecessary.

A popular and spectacular walk is from Hunter's Inn to Woody Bay and back. Here there is an upper and lower path, enabling a circular route. The lower path passes through Hollow Brook, the West Country's highest waterfall, and the upper path gives access to the Roman signal station at Martinhoe. Spectacular views can also be had from the scenic drive at Selworthy Beacon. An exhilarating walk is from the car park down through the woods to Lynch Combe, around Bossington Hill and back along the trail over the Beacon. For sheer atmosphere, however, you cannot beat the wooded stretch between Ashley Combe and the Foreland and the paths to the shore at Embelle and Glenthorne. This is the longest, remotest and most strenuous part of the trail, but it rewards both the time and effort.

RIDING

Exmoor has been described as 'the riding playground of England' and, as a potential National Park, the Hobhouse Report of 1947 cited it as the one best suited for riding. There are over 400 miles (650km) of well-maintained bridleways, which include most of the rights of way across open moorland. Riding stables are scattered over the whole area, and most larger settlements around Exmoor have their vet, tack shop and farrier. The area can offer something to suit most types of rider and there are facilities for hunting, hacking, jumping and trekking, along with indoor schools. Horses can be hired or stabling offered for your horse, often alongside your accommodation. Some establishments offer complete riding holidays, including accommodation and instruction or hire of horses. A list of riding establishments can be found in the *Exmoor Visitor* newspaper, available from the National Park Authority.

CYCLING

Cycling is an up and coming activity on Exmoor, despite the hills. Most visitors drive up the hills to find more level places for cycling. Particularly good for this is the scenic drive between North Hill and Selworthy Beacon and the moorland road between Whitstones on Porlock Hill and Chetsford Bridge or Larkbarrow. There

FOLLOW THE ARROW

There are parts of Exmoor where, partly through the hunting interest, it is common practice to wander freely on horseback, but many local riders have arrangements with the landowners and because you see others riding away from rights of way, it does not mean anyone can. It is wise to take an escort for moorland rides. The British Horse Society has produced a guide to circular trails for riders as part of their Access and Rights of Way (ARROW) strategy. These are particularly suited to those who bring their own horses to Exmoor and the Society also produces a guide to Bed and Breakfast for Horses.

Above: On the National Cycle Route across West Anstey Common

are also some scenic valley routes such as the Exe valley between Winsford and Dulverton, the Washford River between Luxborough and Roadwater, and the broad Vale of Porlock. Part of the National Millennium Cycle Route passes along the southern edge of Exmoor, between Dulverton and Bratton Fleming. It offers superb views from relatively quiet and level roads and has the added convenience of artistic benches at rest points. Most accommodation is around the fringes of the National Park, and one or two accommodation providers offer a service whereby cyclists can be driven up onto the moors from where they are given scenic routes to cycle back.

With off-road cycling, however, the hills are an attraction for the challenge they offer. Despite the gears on mountain bikes, this still calls for a certain level of fitness. Many cyclists are unsure as to where they are allowed to cycle. A basic rule is you cannot cycle freely on moorland without permission. You must keep to the routes which are marked on Ordnance Survey maps as roads, roads used as public paths (RUPPs) or public bridleways. Confusion may arise over permitted routes where some are permitted for riders but not cyclists and vice versa. Both cyclists and riders share the extensive network of bridleways and minor roads on Exmoor, and cyclists need to be aware of the sensitivities of horses and approach them with care. There are leaflets for designated cycle routes around the Crown Estate's woods to the south of Dunster starting at Nutcombe Bottom, on South West Water's property at Wimbleball Lake, starting at Cowling's recreation area, and on North Hill and the Holnicote Estate. These offer off-road cycling routes for all abilities.

WATERSPORTS

Sailing and boating along the Exmoor coast is popular but somewhat limited by the great tidal range. Harbours dry up at low tide, so sailing largely takes place around high tide. Many sailors do the rounds of the Bristol Channel harbours, sailing on one high tide and arriving at their destination on the next. Combe Martin, Lynmouth and Porlock Weir are the harbours within the National Park, with Minehead close by. There are boats for hire at these places and there are regular sightseeing trips from Lynmouth in summer. A popular trip is under the Valley of Rocks to the cliffs at Martinhoe, where there are seabird colonies in spring and early summer.

When the wind is not good for surfing on North Devon's Atlantic beaches, surfers often find that it is better at Lynmouth. Here the shallow delta brings surf into the river mouth at low tide. As well as surf boarding, surf canoeing and wave skiing are also popular. Lynmouth also attracts jet skiers, who can launch easily from the harbour and gain lift from the waves at the river mouth. There are no hire facilities at present.

Kayaking on Exmoor rivers is a popular activity for groups. Special arrangements with river owners and owners of fishing rights mean that river canoeing is by permit only and confined to winter months, when there is enough water and

there is no fishing. Then the rivers are fast flowing and suitable for experienced canoeists only. The Barle between Tarr Steps and Dulverton is the main stretch used. There is also limited canoeing on the East Lyn below Watersmeet. This is both difficult and dangerous but thrilling for those who enjoy the extreme side of the sport.

Sea kayaking is undoubtedly one of the best ways of seeing the remoter parts of the Exmoor coastline in summer. Again, it is an activity for the more experienced and, for safety reasons, best tackled in a group. The coastline is generally sheltered but conditions can quickly change and make it difficult to return to where you set out. Combe Martin, Lynmouth, Porlock Weir and Minehead are places where it is possible to park and unload kayaks close to the beach. Tidal currents in the

SETTING SAIL

Sailboarding on Exmoor waters is mainly confined to Wimbleball Lake, which is popular for most watersports, including sailing and canoeing. These are controlled through the Wimbleball Sailing Club and take place at times when a safety boat is available. Temporary membership is possible and the address can be found at the back of the book.

Above: Sailing boats at Wimbleball Sailing Club
Left: Sailboarding at Wimbleball Lake

Bristol Channel are strong, and it is best to plan journeys so that outward and return parts run with the tide. Keeping close to the shore avoids the excesses of wind and current and in calm conditions it is fun to weave in and out of rocks and caves at high tide. The sheer immensity of the cliffs can only be appreciated from below and this is undoubtedly one of the best ways of seeing Exmoor at its most spectacular.

CLIMBING

Exmoor's soaring sea cliffs may look tempting to the climber but they mostly consist of loose, fragile rock providing few safe climbs. The landowner's permission should be sought before climbing. Some climbs have been documented but most are best known to locals and it is wise to contact local climbing clubs. There is no climbing inland.

Most coastal climbs have the added danger of the possibility of being trapped by a rising tide or falling on slippery rocks. It has been estimated that it would take five years to traverse the whole of the Exmoor coastline at the base of the cliffs, waiting for the right tidal conditions. The climbing is extreme, and the number of people who have completed the traverse can be numbered on one hand. However, a number of enthusiastic locals undertake coasteering – a sport which is gaining in popularity. This usually takes place at low spring tides and involves abseiling down to a remote part of the coast, traversing the base of the cliffs as far as possible by scrambling, climbing or swimming, and climbing back up. Parts of the Exmoor coast are among the most remote in Britain and this is definitely the sport for those with a sense of adventure.

Below: Canoeing on the River Barle
Opposite: Artists at Malmsmead Ford

SWIMMING

As far as the seas around Britain go, the waters of the Bristol Channel are relatively warm. This is partly because of the Gulf Stream drift and partly because of the locking of water within the channel, giving it time to warm up in summer. Sandy beaches and surf are generally lacking on the Exmoor coast, where the beaches are of rock and shingle and sheltered. Exmoor beaches, however, have much more of interest. You can swim from rock to rock and explore the rock pools, and the swimming is safe unless you swim far out where there are tidal currents. The other advantage of Exmoor beaches is that they are never crowded. The main disadvantage is that the tall cliffs shade the beaches and you may have to move around with the sun. The most popular bathing beaches are at Combe Martin and Lee Bay, near Lynton. Others, at Wild Pear, Heddon's Mouth, Woody Bay, Wringcliff Bay and Sillery Sands require long walks or steep climbs and sometimes the paths are washed away. However, seclusion is the reward, which is why such beaches attract naturists!

FISHING

There is no coarse fishing within the National Park, but Exmoor is a paradise for the game fisherman. The Exe, Barle and East Lyn are salmon rivers and many others provide good fly fishing for migratory and brown trout and grayling. All Exmoor rivers are clean and provide good spawning grounds. As elsewhere in Britain, runs of salmon are declining, particularly the spring run, but the Environment Agency is helping to keep stocks up. The West Lyn, Oare Water, Horner Water, Haddeo, Mole and Bray are fished for brown trout. Although rel-

Below: Fly fishing in the Barle at Landacre

atively small, these fish provide good sport and tasty eating. Rainbow and hybrid trout can be found at private fisheries and at Wimbleball Lake. Most freshwater fishing requires a licence and usually an owner's permit as well. Several local fishing tackle shops and others sell licences and details can be found in the National Park Authority's *Exmoor Visitor* newspaper.

Although there is little commercial sea fishing from the Exmoor coast, the area is popular with rod fishermen. Boats from Combe Martin, Lynmouth, Porlock Weir and Minehead take groups along the coast and arrangements can be made to hire a boat or join a trip. Boat owners will often provide tackle, bait and advice. Summer trips for mackerel are particularly popular. The mackerel are usually caught by spinning or feathering, or simply by towing a lure behind the boat. This is very productive but some give the fish more of a sporting chance. Porlock Bay is good for boat fishing and occasionally special trips are made in autumn for tope.

ACCESS FOR DISABLED PEOPLE

Hilly areas like Exmoor are not best suited to those who have mobility problems. However, everyone will find a welcome on Exmoor and many efforts have been made to provide facilities for the disabled. *Accessible Exmoor*- a guide to such facilities – can be obtained from National Park Visitor Centres. This lists a full range of accommodation from hotels, through guest houses to self catering and camping establishments which have special facilities. Most of the major tourist attractions in the area cater for the disabled to some degree, as do the visitor centres. There is an 'Easybus' route from Barnstaple to Lynton and many local minibuses and taxis have special facilities and trained staff.

There are many activities which can be undertaken by the disabled. The Calvert Trust provides multi-activity holidays for disabled people and their families at Wistlandpound on the edge of the moor. At Wimbleball Lake, fishing is possible from a pontoon or specially adapted boat and the Wimbleball Sailing Club has two trimarans adapted for wheelchair users. Several riding centres in and around the National Park offer special facilities and there are horse-drawn cart rides and teaching for pony-drawn carriages. Several short walks are wheelchair accessible, including part of 'Snowdrop Valley' near Wheddon Cross, and there are specially designed wheelchair routes at Selworthy Beacon, Webber's Post and Robber's Bridge.

THOSE 'SPECIAL' QUALITIES

Part of the purposes of National Parks is that they are to be enjoyed for their special qualities such as tranquillity, wildness and remoteness. As Exmoor is one of the least busy and least spoilt National Parks, such qualities are never far away, yet visitors can congregate like bees around a hive at some attractions, which are then known as 'honeypots.' Exmoor villages such as Lynmouth and Dunster are probably the main attractions and few countryside areas become congested. However, it is best to avoid well known places such as Tarr Steps, Landacre Bridge, Watersmeet and Hunter's Inn on Bank Holidays.

Many popular attractions are best visited early or late in the day and these are definitely the times to see wildlife, red deer in particular. In the summer you can see the sun both rise and set over the sea from parts of the coast. To sit and watch the ever-changing light of a sunset in the stillness of Selworthy Beacon, Countisbury or Little Hangman is a memorable experience. To watch the night sky without the distraction of town lighting can also be awesome. Places like

Above: Boardwalk for wheelchair users at Robber's Bridge

Winsford Hill or Molland Moor, where you can see for miles across sparsely populated mid-Devon to Dartmoor, are the best for this. At times there are dawn and evening guided walks specifically designed for watching wildlife, including 'bat walks'.

For wildness and closeness to nature you cannot beat the uninhabited parts of the Exmoor coastline. Access to the shore, however, is usually difficult and often dangerous. You can also find peace almost anywhere in the Brendon Hills. On Croydon Hill you can lose yourself on miles of forest tracks, have stunning open views from Black Hill and Rodhuish Common, and not see another soul all day.

But for the feeling of openness and huge skyscapes, the stretch of boggy, tussocky grass moor between Alderman's Barrow and Brendon Two Gates, takes some beating. Here it is still possible to see for miles all around, without a sign of habitation or modern life.

Right: Exmoor wilderness - Brendon Common

6 Exploring the Park

ALLERFORD

Allerford is a hamlet in Selworthy parish on the National Trust's Holnicote Estate. A picturesque and much photographed fifteenth-century packhorse bridge spans Aller Brook. The old, thatched school is now the West Somerset Rural Life Museum. There is a working smithy, shop, small car park and toilets. Nearby is Piles Mill, a National Trust study centre with the mill open to the public.

BARBROOK

A village in Lynton and Lynmouth parish. There is a memorial to those who lost their lives there in the 1952 flood disaster. To the east is the notorious Beggars Roost Hill, a steep and stony track long used for motor trials.

BLACKMOOR GATE

This is a busy crossroads at the junction of the A39 and A399 named after the former landowners, the Blackmore family, which included the Exmoor novelist, R. D. Blackmore. The former station on the Lynton and Barnstaple Railway is now an inn, and there is a car park, toilets and picnic area.

BOSSINGTON

A picturesque hamlet in Selworthy parish, on the National Trust's Holnicote Estate. Distinctive cottages with chimney stacks and bread ovens bulging from the façades line the single street. There are good walks along the Coast Path to Hurlstone Point and Porlock Marsh and superb views from Bossington Hill. There is a car park, toilets, picnic area and tea gardens in season, and a farm park and medieval chapel at nearby Lynch.

BRENDON

This large parish (population, with Countisbury, 209) includes the heathland of Brendon Common. The village straggles along the East Lyn valley with the church nearly two miles away. The church was moved from Cheriton in the eighteenth century and is dedicated to St Brendan, the much-travelled Irish saint who is reputed to have discovered North America.

BRENDON HILL

Here are remains of the once prosperous iron mining industry, including a miners' chapel at Beulah and ruins of mines, cottages and the steep mineral railway incline running down to Comberow. Car parking is at a lay-by near Ralegh's Cross and it is necessary to explore on foot. Access to Burrow Farm engine house is from near the Naked Boy prehistoric standing stone along the edge of the track bed of the former mineral railway.

Right: Lank Combe Water meets Badgworthy Water in the heart of Doone Country

BRIDGETOWN

Bridgetown is a hamlet alongside the River Exe on the A369, which includes an old mill, packhorse bridge and a cricket pitch with a thatched pavilion. A peaceful

Above: Bridge and ford crossing the Haddeo at Bury

walk leads along the river towards Winsford. Parking is in a lay-by from which a bridge crosses to the cricket pitch. There is a pub and rock faces carved with the dates when the turnpike was cut along the valley in the 1820s.

BROMPTON REGIS

A large parish (pop 407) extending from the Haddeo valley up to the ridge of the Brendon Hills. It includes Wimbleball Lake (see p106), the village of Withiel Florey and the hamlets of Bury and Gupworthy. This quiet village has a pub, shop and tea rooms and nearby is the restored Pulhams Mill with craft workshop.

BURY

Bury is best known for its picturesque bridge and ford, but it is best not to attempt to cross either with a vehicle. It is a good starting point for walks up the beautiful Haddeo valley to Wimbleball Lake or up the rough, old and sunken Haddon Lane to Haddon Hill.

THE CHAINS

A wild moorland ridge with its highest point at Chains Barrow – 1,599ft (487m). A path leads along the southern edge of the ridge between Exe Head and Pinkworthy Pond, which dams the headwaters of the River Barle. The pond was created for landowner John Knight around 1830 but its purpose is unknown. Here is Exmoor's most extensive area of blanket bog; typical plants include deer sedge, cotton grasses, cross-leaved heath, bog asphodel, sundew and heath spotted orchid. Access is usually via the B3358 west of Simonsbath and Shallowford south of Barbrook.

CHAPMAN BARROWS

This collection of 11 barrows which form Exmoor's largest group of Bronze Age burial mounds. They lie mostly on Challacombe Common, known locally as Homer Common. An agreement with the landowner gives access on foot along the Bronze Age ridgeway to Exmoor's tallest standing stone, the Longstone, and to Longstone Barrow. On a clear day you can see most of North Devon, Bodmin Moor and three more National Parks: Dartmoor, Brecon Beacons and the Pembrokeshire Coast. Access is via a long track up from Parracombe or along the wild Chains ridge.

Below: Seaside at Combe Martin

CLOUTSHAM

Cloutsham is a working farm on the National Trust's Holnicote estate. It was a hunting lodge of the Acland family, designed in the ornate rustic style popular on estates in the late eighteenth and early nineteenth centuries. It looks over Cloutsham Woods to the northern slopes of Dunkery Hill, and the meadows near a ford in the woods are popular for picnics. The nearest parking is at Webber's Post to the east or Stoke Ridge to the west and the road through the valley is narrow, winding and precipitous.

COMBE MARTIN

Combe Martin (pop 2,451) is a classic linear settlement, reputedly having the country's longest village street. Characteristic 'sunken lanes' cut into the valley sides away from the street to the medieval strip fields and sites of former silver mines. Lying mostly outside the National Park, the village provides many services, including shops, cafes, restaurants, bank, health centre and National Park Visitor Centre. The beach and nearby Wild Pear Beach have great geological interest and lie within the National Park.

*Below: County Gate and Yenworthy
Common from Cosgate Hill
Opposite: Looking down Countisbury
Hill towards Lynton, Lynmouth and
the Lyn delta (courtesy National
Trust)*

COUNTISBURY

A tiny hilltop settlement with a church, old coaching inn and car park. There are superb walks on the Foreland, with views down Countisbury Hill to Lynmouth, to the Iron Age rampart on Wind Hill, and along the cleave above the spectacular wooded East Lyn gorge.

COUNTY GATE

Set on a windy ridge between the East Lyn valley and the Bristol Channel on the A39 between Devon and Somerset. The old gatehouse is now a National Park Visitor Centre with car park and toilets. There are views to Doone Country and this is a good starting point for exploring that area or the Glenthorne Estate, with steep trails to a pinetum and stony beach with fascinating geology.

COW CASTLE

An Iron Age fort spectacularly situated on top of a natural hillock in the Barle valley. It is on a popular walk running along the bottom and side of the valley between Simonsbath and Braddymoor.

CULBONE

Culbone church, dedicated to St Beuno, is reputed to be the smallest parish church in England. It has Saxon parts and there are many legends surrounding its ancient

history. The cottages, formerly part of the Lovelace estate based at Ashley Combe, are in the style of Voysey. Its chief charm is its setting – deep in a shady, wooded combe on the side of the Bristol Channel – and was inspiration for Coleridge's *Kubla Khan*. There are no public roads to the village and access is via the Coast Path from Porlock Weir or the toll road at Ashley Combe.

Above: Oare church: the setting for Lorna Doone's wedding in Blackmore's novel

DOONE COUNTRY

The area centred around Badgworthy Water is famed as home of the legendary Doones, a family of seventeenth-century outlaws. Legend placed the Doones in the deserted medieval settlement in Hoccombe Combe, a tributary of Badgworthy. The valley of Blackmore's famous novel *Lorna Doone*, however, more closely resembled Lank Combe, another tributary. A visit to both combes requires a 5-mile (8km) walk from Malmsmead. Badgworthy Water marks the boundary between Devon and Somerset and runs through beautiful heathland and an ancient woodland of crooked oaks. There is a car park, toilets and natural history centre at Malmsmead, and teas are available in season at Malmsmead or Cloud Farm. One mile along a riverside walk from Malmsmead is the tiny church at Oare where Lorna Doone married Jan Ridd, the hero of the novel.

DULVERTON

A busy little town (pop 1,347) acting as a service centre for southern Exmoor. It lies in an attractive setting where the deep and wooded Barle valley broadens into meadows before joining the Exe. A medieval bridge spans the river near the former workhouse, now the National Park Authority's offices. There is a National Park Visitor Centre adjoining the Heritage Centre, which has an art gallery and displays about Dulverton and the surrounding woodlands. There are many shops and services, including bank, chemist, library and health centre. Early closing is on Thursday.

DUNKERY HILL

A large hill which forms the highest part of Exmoor's central ridge. It has a chain of summits capped with Bronze Age barrows, at Rowbarrows, Kit Barrows, Robin How and Dunkery Beacon, Exmoor's highest point at 1,705ft (519m). There are easy walks to the summit from informal car parks at Dunkery Gate and Rex Stile Head. The Beacon was the site of a former fire beacon and is still occasionally used for celebratory bonfires. A cairn commemorating the giving of the area to the National Trust and a toposcope (viewfinder) mark the summit. There are extensive all-round views on clear days.

DUNSTER

Dunster (pop 948) is one of the most visited places on Exmoor. It has all the features you would expect of an English medieval village, including an ancient castle, priory, dovecote, yarn market, inn, packhorse bridge and mill – plus the modern scourge of busy road traffic. Its once prosperous woollen industry died in the eighteenth century, since when the village has been locked in a time warp. The main attraction is the National Trust castle, former home of the Luttrell family. However, the whole village and the lush countryside surrounding it are equally worth exploration. The National Park Visitor Centre shares displays with the National Trust and the Crown Estate, the major landowners in the area. Services are mainly tourist oriented, with a plethora of gift and tea shops.

Below: The Yarn Market and castle face each other along Dunster's High Street

EXFORD

Exford (pop 399) is an attractive village set around a green. It acts as a service centre for central Exmoor, and its tourism is mainly based on hunting and riding.

HORNER

This hamlet in Luccombe parish has tea gardens and is convenient for the beautiful walks along Horner Water. The woods form part of a National Nature Reserve, a stronghold for red deer, and contain ancient pollarded oaks with rare lichens.

HUNTER'S INN

Hunter's Inn is set in a picturesque location in the deep, wooded Heddon Valley. There is a National Trust Visitor Centre, car park and toilets. There are relatively level paths forming a popular walk either side of the river to the small, rocky beach and lime kiln at Heddon's Mouth.

LANDACRE BRIDGE

This medieval bridge spans the River Barle, where it runs through Withypool Common. The combination of water, moorland and resident Exmoor ponies make it and nearby Sherdon Hutch popular picnic sites for locals. There is no formal parking or facilities and can be a haphazard 'free for all' on busy days.

LARKBARROW

The ruins of this isolated farm were used for firing practice during World War II. It is surrounded by miles of open, rolling grass moorland, and is one of the best places to experience remoteness and tranquillity on Exmoor. A track runs through from Alderman's Barrow or Larkbarrow Corner to Badgworthy Water, and there is open access to this boggy and tussocky terrain.

LEE BAY

A small, rocky and sheltered bathing beach, popular with visitors to Lynton and Lynmouth. It is part of the Lee Abbey estate and there is a charge for the toll road and car park. There are toilets, a tea garden in season, a small natural history museum and an unusual chapel in a former lime kiln.

Top: Exford's village green
Above: Morris dancing at Hunter's Inn
Opposite: Heddon's Mouth: a popular walk from Hunter's Inn (courtesy National Trust)

LUCCOMBE

Luccombe (pop 173) is a pretty National Trust village of old cottages, with a beautiful church and thatched shop.

LUXBOROUGH

Luxborough (pop 201) is a scattered village with pub, church and car park. It is a good centre for exploring the forested parts of the Brendon Hills, with walks over the Chargot estate to Kennisham, over Croydon Hill to the deserted village of Clicket, or across the open heaths of Withycombe and Rodhuish Commons.

LYNMOUTH

Lynmouth is probably the busiest attraction in the National Park, but the tourism is seasonal and winter is quiet. Its attraction derives chiefly from its spectacular setting at the mouths of the wooded gorges of the East and West Lyn rivers, hemmed in by gigantic cliffs. Few sit on the pebbly beach but jet skiing, boat trips and surfing are popular when conditions are favourable. There are many gift shops and eating places, a National Park Visitor Centre, two museums to the 1952 flood disaster which made the village famous, and the equally famous cliff railway to Lynton.

LYNTON

The National Park's main town (pop with Lynmouth, 1,658) and service centre with a variety of facilities including plenty of car parking. The buildings are mainly Victorian, of local stone and terracotta roof tiles and a variety of architectural designs, including Swiss-style balconies and carved barge boards. The Lyn and Exmoor Museum has a collection devoted to Exmoor's social history.

Above: Cottages at the head of Stoney Street, Luccombe
Opposite: Lynmouth: famous for its flood disaster
Below: Nettlecombe Court and church from the Park

MONKSILVER

An attractive village (pop 103) which straddles the National Park boundary. Nearby is Combe Sydenham country park, with a sixteenth-century house which was home of Elizabeth Sydenham, second wife of Sir Francis Drake. There are pleasant walks over rolling farmland to Nettlecombe Park and superb views from Bird's Hill.

NETTLECOMBE

Nettlecombe (pop 180) is a scattered settlement with a beautiful church and a sixteenth-century court, once the home of the Trevellyan family and now a study centre. The park contains superb old oak trees and is a Site of Special Scientific Interest.

NORTH HILL

North Hill overlooks Minehead, with superb views across the Bristol Channel. The coastal heath is a blaze of colour in August. At Moor Wood are the remains of a World War II tank training ground and radar station. Here also is a car park, picnic area and the starting point for numerous walks.

NUTCOMBE BOTTOM

A car park and picnic area with access for the disabled and centre for walks and mountain bike rides around the Crown Estate's forested hills to the south of Dunster. The Douglas firs in nearby Broadwood are Britain's tallest stand of trees, and there are superb views over Dunster and the coast from Bat's Castle Iron Age fort.

PARRACOMBE

Parracombe (pop 310) is a village boasting an inn, shop and two churches. The ancient St Petrock's church is now redundant, but retains a perfectly preserved eighteenth-century interior.

PORLOCK

Porlock (pop 1,332) is an attractive village with old thatched cottages and a mixture of other buildings. It is also a local service centre with a range of shops and facilities, including a modern visitor centre. Worth a visit are the ancient parish church dedicated to St Dubricius and the museum based in the medieval manorial dower house. Porlock Hill, notorious for its steepness, can be by-passed by a toll road. It crosses the heathland of Porlock Common, from where there are beautiful views to Porlock Bay and Dunkery.

PORLOCK WEIR

A picturesque hamlet and former working harbour, enclosed by lock gates. The gates are now used mainly to flush pebbles from the harbour entrance, which cuts through the shingle ridge. Porlock Weir is on the Coast Path and a starting point for walks to Culbone or Porlock Marsh. There is a car park, toilets, pub, restaurant and shops.

ROBBER'S BRIDGE

A popular picnic spot on Weir Water, accessible via a narrow, steep and winding road from the A39 near the top of Porlock Hill or the equally narrow road from Oare. There is a tiny road bridge, reputed to be the site of a Doone robbery. A path and short boardwalk for wheelchairs runs from a car park over private ground by agreement with the landowner.

SELWORTHY

Selworthy (pop 518) is a village famed for its thatched cottages, mostly in National Trust ownership but privately tenanted. The beautiful whitewashed church overlooks a green where there is a National Trust shop, toilets and a tea shop. There are miles of walks on the wooded hillside behind, with superb views across the Vale of Porlock and along the coast from Selworthy Beacon, where there is a wheelchair trail.

SIMONSBATH

A nineteenth-century village created by the Knight family, who bought the area from the Crown as part of the former Royal Forest of Exmoor. There is a car park, toilets and picnic area at Ashcombe. It is a popular starting point for walks along the River Barle and the meadow by the river is also popular for picnics. There is a pub, shop and tea rooms.

Left: The heathland of Porlock Common offers beautiful views to Porlock Bay

Above: Tarr Steps: Britain's largest clapper bridge
Right: The East Lyn and Hoaroak Water meet at Watersmeet (courtesy National Trust)

TARR STEPS

This ancient 'clapper' bridge across the River Barle is a popular tourist attraction, which should be avoided at peak times. The bridge is of primitive construction, with large unmortared slabs of stone resting on one another, and is the largest example of its type. Its age and history are unknown, except for the fact that it has been restored several times in recent years, following flood damage. The river and the valley woodlands are Sites of Special Scientific Interest and abound with wildlife. Pleasant footpaths run along the valley between Simonsbath and Dulverton. Car park and toilets are on a narrow road 400yd/m from the bridge. Parking for the disabled and refreshments are available nearer the bridge.

THE VALLEY OF ROCKS

This rocky valley to the west of Lynton is arguably the most spectacular scenic location on Exmoor. There are many legends surrounding the rock formations, the remains of prehistoric settlement and the herd of wild goats. It is reached by an easy walk from Lynton, along Lee Road or North Walk, part of the Coast Path. Public footpaths around the valley provide spectacular views, particularly from South Cliff and Hollerday Hill. There are toilets and refreshments in season.

WATERSMEET

Watersmeet is a popular beauty spot at the junction of the East Lyn and Hoaroak Water. The rivers flow through deep wooded gorges with numerous footpaths and bridges, all well maintained by the National Trust. The Trust has a visitor centre and tea gardens at a former nineteenth-century fishing lodge with access for disabled visitors (by appointment) and toilets. Otherwise there is a short but steep

walk down from the car park on the A39 or a mile and a half walk up river from Lynmouth. The gorge is a Site of Special Scientific Interest and there are rare ferns, flowers and trees.

WEBBER'S POST

Named after a huntsman and once a meeting point for staghounds, Webber's Post is now a popular car park and viewpoint. There are views over Horner Woods to Cloutsham and Dunkery. The National Trust has provided a wheelchair trail through self-seeded pine trees on the ridge alongside the East Water valley.

WIMBLEBALL LAKE

One of the West Country's largest reservoirs, managed by South West Water and supplying a large part of Devon and Somerset. The 161ft (50m) high dam runs across the River Haddeo, a tributary of the Exe. It is accessible on foot from Haddon Hill, where there is a car park, toilets, heathland walks and Exmoor ponies. There is also a car park at Bessom Bridge at the northern end of the lake, where there is a nature reserve. The main facilities are at Cowlings, where there is a recreation area, refreshments (in season), fishing and sailing (via the Wimbleball Sailing Club). Paths extend for about 10 miles (16 km) around most of the lake shore.

WINSFORD

Winsford (pop 270) is a pretty village with several bridges and a ford over the Winn Brook and River Exe. There is a garage, shop, toilets, tea garden and a popular thatched pub.

WINSFORD HILL

Winsford Hill is a heath-covered common, managed by the National Trust. The three Bronze Age Wambarrows mark the highest point, with good views to Dunkery, Dartmoor and the Blackdown Hills. It is a popular place to see the pure-bred Exmoor ponies of the well-known Anchor herd. At Spire Cross there is a standing stone is inscribed 'Caratacus Nepus', which means a relative of Caratacus, possibly the British leader who resisted the Roman invasion. However, the stone appears to have been inscribed centuries after his death. It once lay broken but now has a small shelter to protect it.

WITHYPOOL

Withypool (pop 196) is a small village with pub, shop and toilets in a beautiful setting overlooking the Barle valley and heathland of Withypool Common.

WOODY BAY

The hamlet of Woody Bay was once destined as a tourist resort, but it is now a quiet residential area. A steep track runs to a rough slipway and a small beach with a lime kiln, lime burner's cottage and the remains of a pier. Hanging Water stream runs down thickly wooded cliffs to a waterfall, and there are legends of ghosts, probably put about by smugglers. A car park high above the beach gives access to the Coast Path.

Right: Haddon Hill provides views over Wimbleball Lake and the surrounding Brendon Hills

Information

USEFUL ADDRESSES

Exmoor National Park Authority
Exmoor House
Dulverton
Somerset
TA22 9HL
Tel: 01398 323665

Council for National Parks
246 Lavender Hill
London SW11 1LJ
Tel: 020 7924 5761

Devon Wildlife Trust
Shirehampton House
35-37 St David's Hill
Exeter
Devon
EX4 4DA
Tel: 01392 279244

English Heritage
Fortress House
23 Saville Row
London
W1X 2HE
Tel: 0171 973 3434

English Nature
Roughmoor
Bishop's Hull
Taunton
Somerset
TA1 5AA
Tel: 01823 283211

Environment Agency
Manley House
Kestrel Way
Exeter
Devon
EX2 7LQ
Tel: 01392 444000

Exmoor Natural History Society
c/o Miss C. Giddens
12 King George Road
Minehead
Somerset
TA24 5JD
Tel: 01643 707624

Exmoor Society
Parish Rooms
Rosemary Lane
Dulverton
Somerset
TA22 9BR
Tel: 01398 323335

Field Studies Council
The Leonard Wills Field Centre
Nettlecombe Court
Williton
Taunton
Somerset
TA4 4HT
Tel: 01984 640320

Forestry Commission
District Office for North Devon and
Cornwall
Cooksworthy Moor
Beaworthy
Devon
EX21 5UK
Tel: 01409 221692

Forestry Commission
District Office for Somerset and
South Devon
Bullers Hill,
Kennford
Exeter
Devon
EX6 7ER
Tel: 01392 832262

National Trust
Devon Regional Office
Killerton House
Broadclyst
Exeter
EX5 3LE
Tel: 01392 881691

Royal Society for the Protection of
Birds
Keble House
Southernhay Gardens
Exeter
Devon
EX1 1NT
Tel: 01392 432691

Somerset Wildlife Trust
Fyne Court
Broomfield
Bridgwater
Somerset
TA5 2EQ
Tel: 01278 451587

South West Water
Leisure Services
Higher Coombepark
Lewdown
Okehampton
Devon
EX20 4QT
Tel: 01837 871565

Youth Hostels Association
Southern England Regional Office
11B York Road
Salisbury
Wiltshire
SP2 7AP
Tel: 01722 337515

Attractions

Allerford Rural Life Museum
The Old School
Allerford
Minehead
Somerset
TA24 8HN
Tel: 01643 862529

Arlington Court (National Trust)
Shirwell
Barnstaple
Devon
EX31 4LP
Tel: 01271 850296

Calvert Trust
Wistlandpound
Kentisbury
Barnstaple
Devon
EX31 4SJ
Tel: 01598 763221

Combe Sydenham Country Park
Monksilver
Taunton
Somerset
TA4 4JG
Tel: 01984 656284

Dunster Castle (National Trust)
Dunster
Minehead
Somerset
TA24 6SL
Tel: 01643 821314

Holnicote Estate Office (National
Trust)
Selworthy
Minehead
Somerset
TA24 8TJ
Tel: 01643 862452

Lyn and Exmoor Museum
St Vincent's Cottage
Market Street
Lynton
Devon
EX35 6AF
Tel: 01598 752317

Wimbleball Sailing Club
c/o Mr G. Bass
35 Oakfield Park
Wellington
Somerset
Tel: 01823 474531

Tourist Information Centres

West Country Tourist Board
networked centres offering
accommodation booking services for
personal callers:

Combe Martin TIC
Seacot, 13 Cross Street
Combe Martin
Devon
Tel: 01271 883319
(open April-October)

Lynton and Lynmouth TIC
Town Hall
Lee Road
Lynton
Devon
Tel: 01598 752225
(open all year)

Minehead and West Somerset TIC
17 Friday Street
Minehead
Somerset
Tel: 01643 702624
(open all year)

South Molton TIC
1 East Street
South Molton
Devon
Tel: 01769 574122
(open all year)

Visitor Centres

Porlock Visitor Centre
West End
High Street
Porlock
Somerset
Tel: 01643 863150

National Park Visitor Centres

Combe Martin
Seacot
Cross Street
Combe Martin
Devon
Tel: 01271 883319
(open April-October)

County Gate
On the A39
Countisbury
Lynton
Devon
Tel: 01598 741321
(open April-October)

Dulverton
Fore Street
Dulverton
Somerset
Tel: 01398 323841
(open all year)

Dunster
Dunster Steep
Dunster
Minehead
Somerset
Tel: 01643 821835
(open April-October, limited winter
opening)

Lynmouth
The Esplanade
Lynmouth
Devon
Tel: 01598 752509
(open April-October)

FURTHER READING

Blackmore, R.D. *Lorna Doone* (Sampson Low, 1869)

Binding, Hilary (ed) *The Changing Face of Exmoor* (Exmoor Books, 1995)

Binding, Hilary *Enjoying Exmoor* (Exmoor Books, 1999)

Bourne, Hope L. *Living on Exmoor* (Galley Press, 1963)

Burton, S.H. *Exmoor* (Hodder and Stoughton, 1969)

Butler, D. *Ranger's Favourite Walks* (Exmoor Books, 1999)

Eardley-Wilmot, Hazel *Yesterday's Exmoor* (Exmoor Books, 1990)

Exmoor Natural History Society *The Fauna and Flora of Exmoor National Park* (Exmoor Books, 1996)

Lawrence, Berta *Exmoor Villages* (Exmoor Press, 1984)

MacDermot, E.T. *A History of the Forest of Exmoor* (David & Charles, 1973)

Orwin, C.S., Sellick, R. and Bonham-Carter, V. *The Reclamation of Exmoor Forest* (Exmoor Books, 1997)

Page, J.L.W. *An Exploration of Exmoor* (Seeley and Co, 1890)

Turner, W.J. *Exmoor Village* (Harrap, 1947)

Williamson, H. *The Gale of the World* (Macdonald, 1969)

Yeates, J. *An Endless View: The Artist and Exmoor* (Exmoor Books, 1995)

MAPS

The use of the appropriate Ordnance Survey maps is highly recommended for any detailed exploration of the National Park, especially if you are venturing out into the countryside and leaving the car behind.

Outdoor Leisure Map (1:25,000)
No 9: Exmoor
Touring Map (1 inch to 1 mile)
No 5: Exmoor

Index

Page numbers in *italics* indicate illustrations